Qualitative Longitudinal Methods

Praise for this book

Dr. Derrington covers an area that's often hard to cover, and she does it succinctly and clearly and rigorously. That's what we need in qualitative research endeavors. Instead of spending time apologizing that our methods are not quantitative, spend more time explaining what is we do as qualitative researchers. Derrington communicates it well!

—Tim Atkinson, University of Central Arkansas

The material presented in the book provides information to qualitative researchers interested in conducting longitudinal studies. The information helps researchers build on their qualitative research skills.

—Lydia Kyei-Blankson, Illinois State University

This book explores the intricacies of longitudinal qualitative research. It shares many of the pragmatic concerns centered in this research method. The author provides numerous examples to make this text come alive and provide models for researchers.

—Diane Barone, University of Nevada, Reno

Dr. Mary Lynne Derrington provides clarity of purpose and intent about longitudinal research methods and approaches in a way that supports examining change over time. This is a book that I will use and recommend to others.

—Sally J. Zepeda, University of Georgia

Qualitative Longitudinal Methods

Researching Implementation and Change

Mary Lynne Derrington

*University of Tennessee
at Knoxville*

Los Angeles | London | New Delhi
Singapore | Washington DC | Melbourne

Qualitative Research Methods Series

Series Editor: David L. Morgan, *Portland State University*

The **Qualitative Research Methods Series** currently consists of 54 volumes that address essential aspects of using qualitative methods across social and behavioral sciences. These widely used books provide valuable resources for a broad range of scholars, researchers, teachers, students, and community-based researchers.

The series publishes volumes that:

- Address topics of current interest to the field of qualitative research.
- Provide practical guidance and assistance with collecting and analyzing qualitative data.
- Highlight essential issues in qualitative research, including strategies to address those issues.
- Add new voices to the field of qualitative research.

A key characteristic of the Qualitative Research Methods Series is an emphasis on both a *"why to"* a *"how-to"* perspective, so that readers will understand the purposes and motivations behind a method, as well as the practical and technical aspects of using that method. These relatively short and inexpensive books rely on a cross-disciplinary approach, and they typically include examples from practice; tables, boxes, and figures; discussion questions; application activities; and further reading sources.

New and forthcoming volumes in the Series include:

Qualitative Longitudinal Methods:
Researching Implementation and Change
Mary Lynne Derrington

Qualitative Instrument Design:
A Guide for the Novice Researcher
Felice D. Billups

Hybrid Ethnography:
Online, Offline, and In-between
Liz Przybylski

Photovoice for Social Justice:
Image Capturing in Action
Jean M. Breny and Shannon L. McMorrow

For information on how to submit a proposal for the Series, please contact:

David L. Morgan, Series Editor: morgand@pdx.edu

Leah Fargotstein, Acquisitions Editor, SAGE: leah.fargotstein@sagepub.com

FOR INFORMATION:

SAGE Publications, Inc.
2455 Teller Road
Thousand Oaks, California 91320
E-mail: order@sagepub.com

SAGE Publications Ltd.
1 Oliver's Yard
55 City Road
London EC1Y 1SP
United Kingdom

SAGE Publications India Pvt. Ltd.
B 1/I 1 Mohan Cooperative Industrial Area
Mathura Road, New Delhi 110 044
India

SAGE Publications Asia-Pacific Pte Ltd.
18 Cross Street
#10-10/11/12 China Square Central
Singapore 048423

Acquisitions Editor: Helen Salmon
Editorial Assistant: Megan O'Heffernan
Production Editor: Kimaya Khashnobish
Copy Editor: Diane DiMura
Typesetter: C&M Digitals (P) Ltd.
Proofreader: Lawrence W. Baker
Indexer: Diggs Publication
        Services Pvt Ltd
Cover Designer: Dally Verghese
Marketing Manager: Susannah Goldes

Printed in the United States of America

Library of Congress Cataloging-in-Publication Data

Names: Derrington, Mary Lynne, author.

Title: Qualitative longitudinal methods : researching implementation and change / Mary Lynne Derrington.

Description: Los Angeles : SAGE, 2019. | Includes bibliographical references and index.

Identifiers: LCCN 2018032216 | ISBN 9781506395791 (pbk. : alk. paper)

Subjects: LCSH: Education—Research—Methodology. | Qualitative research. | Longitudinal method.

Classification: LCC LB1028 .D4425 2019 | DDC 370.72—dc23 LC record available at https://lccn.loc.gov/2018032216

This book is printed on acid-free paper.

18 19 20 21 22 10 9 8 7 6 5 4 3 2 1

CONTENTS

PREFACE

WHY I WROTE THIS BOOK

My longitudinal story started years ago when I read a book about creating one's life. Although I no longer remember the title or the author, remaining with me is the concept that a life story, much like longitudinal research, is created over time and influenced by events, both planned and unexpected. Around the time of this epiphany, I became familiar with various stage theories, for example, Gale Sheehy on passages and Elisabeth Kübler-Ross on stages of grief. Although I had yet acquired any research skills, I mentally filed the thought that following individuals over time might lead to theories of transitions and potential understandings of self and others.

I later learned that serendipity can be a wonderful thing while in another life transition. Pursuing a doctorate at the University of Washington, Seattle, I reluctantly enrolled in a research class on historical research methodology. Surprisingly, historical research fascinated me. As I approached my dissertation with the guidance of my chair, Dr. Ann Lieberman, I combined case study methods with my new love of history and focused on a research topic investigating the school principal's evolutionary role. Then Harry F. Wolcott's significant ethnographic work, *The Man in the Principal's Office*, came to my attention. I was a beginning principal at the time and from the title understood that women have a long way to go if only men were viewed as seated in the principal's chair. As I began my research, I understood both the value of longitudinality's long view and the tremendous opportunity for understanding changing perspectives over time. I also realized that understanding could lead to change and to disrupting the status quo.

In the next stage of my career, I served as a school superintendent. An important research-relevant concept I learned on the job was that the inevitability of change requires deep understanding to achieve implementation success. The work of Gene Hall and Shirley Hord introduced me to the Concerns Based Adoption Model (CBAM). Their work solidified my ideas of stage concepts, change, qualitative research methods, and the practicality of applying those concepts to help people in schools implement policies and manage change.

Now in the professoriate, my current life chapter, I understand the importance of longitudinal qualitative research from experience. For six years, I have studied specific reforms related to developing and implementing policies and procedures for teacher evaluation. I have learned many useful lessons from researchers and authors who unbeknownst to them have assisted me in my quest to understand change through qualitative longitudinal research. Although their guidance was wise and helpful, I found gaps in the specifics of conducting qualitative longitudinal research. These gaps led to unanswered questions and subsequently to my own research into this methodology's strategies. As a result, I seek through this book to build a bridge between theory and practice and to share my learning along with the advice of many authors and researchers. My purpose is understanding change. My goal is promoting application of qualitative longitudinal research to accomplish that purpose. Through this book, I hope to convince those unfamiliar with qualitative longitudinal research that managing its challenges are worthwhile.

Unlike the many renowned authors cited in this book, I do not claim to be a methodologist. Instead, I am a researcher and a practitioner who has applied the qualitative longitudinal method to understand thorny and frequently intractable problems of change in education. I am also a translator interpreting the methodologists' expertise for those who wish to see how the method appears in action. Finally, I am a teacher who illustrates with examples for readers to learn the practical application. Change will happen without our research. But with our research and use of the qualitative longitudinal method, the outcome can be a positive step in understanding change and implementing strategies for improvement.

I am indebted to researchers I know and those I have yet to meet. Their advice is included in this book. Their wisdom shared in books and articles influenced my thoughts about qualitative longitudinal research. Their insight assisted me in developing my understanding that I am sharing with readers. My objective is that others will benefit from these collective insights and embrace qualitative longitudinal work.

This book combines qualitative longitudinal sections from articles and books and translates them into action with examples. It will be useful to graduate students planning a dissertation and to early career faculty planning a qualitative longitudinal study. Professors of qualitative methodology courses can also use it as a supplementary teaching resource.

ORGANIZATION OF BOOK

Chapter 1 reviews the basics of qualitative research and explores longitudinality's contribution to qualitative methods. In addition, the management of challenges it explored as well as its benefits in the longitudinal qualitative approach.

Chapter 2 provides a review of qualitative research's design basics. The reader will also learn to include longitudinality into a basic qualitative study design. Useful theoretical change frames are presented with examples of how researchers can incorporate them into studies. In addition, because ethical issues can be magnified in a qualitative longitudinal study, they should be considered early in the study design.

Chapter 3 explores the application of longitudinal methods to many types of qualitative studies including historical, trend, ethnographic, grounded theory, and case studies. The chapter emphasized that all qualitative research seeks to understand how people make meaning of experiences. However, specific considerations in each inquiry method are also important in qualitative longitudinal studies.

Chapter 4 is devoted to a discussion of the researcher–participant relationship from both the researchers' and participants' viewpoints. Multiple ways to demonstrate appreciated of participants' time and involvement are presented. In addition, researchers are cautioned to be aware of how the longer interaction time with participants in a longitudinal qualitative study might also affect the researchers' attitudes, values, and belief systems.

Chapter 5 investigates the usefulness of data-management strategies throughout a qualitative longitudinal study. Advantages and limitations of data-management software programs are discussed in relation to use and storage of a large qualitative data set.

Chapter 6 examines the process of analyzing qualitative longitudinal data. Many examples are presented to assist the researcher in creating a workable method. In addition, a variety of useful techniques illustrate ways to create meaningful visuals.

Chapter 7 focuses on the many factors to consider when preparing a longitudinal qualitative study's results for publication. Creating a meaningful and readable final manuscript is discussed. Also, examples from published studies are presented.

Chapter 8 summarizes lessons learned throughout many studies. This chapter reminds readers of change's centrality in a qualitative longitudinal study. It also emphasizes the importance of leaving a legacy for others to continue the research in a quest for understanding not only change but also the impact on organizations, individuals, and policy.

ACKNOWLEDGMENTS

Many talented people provided support and encouragement while I wrote this book. I am grateful to Linda Blake Walsh, who provided thoughtful critique and editing as I wrote. Throughout the journey, she was a reliable friend and a trusted advisor. I deeply appreciate the insight and creativity of my colleague and friend, John Wilson Campbell. As a current school district leader, he grounds my work in issues significant to principals and teachers today. I am grateful to Cathie Eileen West, my former school colleague and now a respected author. Cathie provided advice and encouraging words when I needed them most. I thank graduate student Jacob Andrew Kamer for contributing a student perspective with a positive attitude and sense of humor. I wish to recognize and thank Helen Salmon, senior acquisitions editor, Megan O'Heffernan, editorial assistant, and all the unsung heroes of the SAGE publishing staff who assisted, frequently in the background, during the book publication process.

The author and SAGE would like to thank the following for their feedback during development:

Tim Atkinson, University of Arkansas

Diana Barone, University of Nevada, Reno

Carla L. Fisher, University of Florida

Valeria J. Freysinger, Miami University

N. Emel Ganapati, Florida International University

Benjamin Henwood, University of Southern California

Ezekiel Kimball, University of Massachusetts, Amherst

Lydia Kyei-Blankson, Illinois State University

Michelle G. Shedlin, NYU Meyers College of Nursing

Sally Zepeda, University of Georgia

ABOUT THE AUTHOR

 **Mary Lynne Derrington** is an associate professor at the University of Tennessee, Knoxville, in the Educational Leadership and Policy Studies Department. Her research has focused on leadership, change, and policy implementation. Her numerous articles and book chapters address perspectives on change and local implementation of state, federal, and international teacher evaluation policies. Mary Lynne regularly presents papers at the annual meetings of the American Educational Research Association and the University Council of Educational Administration. With her work including an international perspective, she has also presented papers at the meetings of the Teacher Education Policy in Europe network, the International Congress for School Effectiveness and Improvement, and the International Study Association on Teachers and Teaching. She is a former school superintendent, principal, and teacher with experience in the American International Schools. Her doctorate is from the University of Washington, Seattle.

THE BENEFITS AND CHALLENGES OF LONGITUDINAL QUALITATIVE STUDIES

In this chapter, the reader will

- review the basics of longitudinal qualitative research,
- explore longitudinality's contribution to qualitative methodologies,
- examine the longitudinal perspective as a way of understanding and describing change, and
- consider the management of challenges in the longitudinal approach.

DESCRIBING LONGITUDINAL RESEARCH

Longitudinal research is about understanding change over time in an individual or a group. Qualitative methodologies include historical, ethnographic, grounded theory, and trend studies. In addition, many methods are possible for data collection; but hallmarks of such research are time, relationships, and change. Regarding the variable of time, "There is no clear definition of the meaning of 'long' in longitudinal research" (Corden & Millar, 2007, p. 586). However, the minimum standard is two or more measurements for one year or longer. The frequency of contacts with participants depends on the study's purpose; there are no set rules. Additionally, measures used, such as repeated interviews, should be comparable, but not necessarily identical. In brief, a longitudinal qualitative study involves making intentional research decisions regarding length of time as well as the reasoning for the specific methodology, participants, and data gathering measures.

The rewards of conducting longitudinal qualitative research have been enumerated by researchers (Corden & Millar, 2007; McLeod & Thomson, 2011; Saldaña, 2003) and in my own research described throughout this book. For example, the researcher develops greater understanding of an issue and establishes an ongoing relationship with participants, resulting in insightful conclusions. However, analyzing a large data set and keeping participants involved over time are challenges for the longitudinal qualitative researcher. While researchers should be interested in their topic, their desire to learn about the topic is imperative for long-term involvement in longitudinal research. Rossman and Rallis (2012) call this desire "Want-to-Do-Ability" (p. 116), referring to the commitment originating from a deep desire to answer the research questions. However, the researcher must ensure that intense desire does not bias the research. These authors also note that the research process involves peaks and valleys of feelings: exhilaration, frustration, difficulty, and boredom. Before further exploring longitudinal approaches, a brief review of qualitative research's key elements will be helpful.

QUALITATIVE BASICS: A REVIEW

In this review, it is impossible to cover thousands of pages in publications written by highly regarded methodologists. Instead, a few key concepts will be highlighted. This review can also serve as a refresher for those who took a course in qualitative methods some time ago. In designing studies, researchers must consider methodologies compatible with their skills and interests. Early in an introductory methods course, students express a preference for qualitative or quantitative research. One typical reason is a hatred or a love of numbers. Another is a preference for the closeness of face-to-face interaction with participants versus the more impersonal quantitative data-collection tools.

A qualitative researcher seeks to understand people from their point of view and within their social and cultural contexts. Different philosophical assumptions (i.e., paradigms) influence how phenomena are studied and understood. This understanding leads to different inquiry strategies (i.e., methodologies) and to different ways (i.e., methods) of gathering and analyzing empirical data.

All qualitative studies involve a researcher orientation frequently labeled using two interchangeable terms: *interpretive* and *constructivist* (Merriam, 2009). A goal for the qualitative researcher is to understand how people interpret their experiences and make sense of their world (Flick, 2014; Merriam, 2009; Merriam & Tisdell, 2016). The qualitative researcher's belief about the nature of knowledge guiding the research and about the nature of reality becomes the epistemology and the ontology embraced (Gall, Gall, & Borg, 2010). *Empiricism* is another concept fundamental to qualitative inquiry and is characterized by the philosophy that knowledge is acquired through direct experience in the field (Rossman & Rallis, 2012). Discussing qualitative research's uniqueness as a method of learning about a field, Rossman and Rallis (2012) emphasize that the researcher is the data-collection instrument in a naturalistic setting. These key principles apply to qualitative research conducted in a variety of social sciences (e.g., nursing, education, psychology, life studies) as well as in the business field.

Qualitative researchers recognize that they bring opinions, assumptions, and preconceptions into a study that might influence the outcome. According to Rossman and Rallis (2012), "Data do not speak for themselves; they are interpreted through complex cognitive processes" (p. 34). Thus, qualitative researchers describe their reflexivity and acknowledge their role and experience in each of a study's stages. Reflexivity in qualitative research requires self-knowledge and reflection so that the assumptions and preconceptions brought into the research and possibly influencing the outcomes are clarified.

Qualitative methods are described as process oriented (Flick, 2014). The qualitative methodology's basic data-collection tools are interviews and observations. In qualitative research, interaction with participants is fundamental. In fact, researchers frequently identify interviewing respondents as the most enjoyable aspect of qualitative research. Qualitative researchers also work with text, making little or no use of numbers or statistics. Reflections, observations, and impressions can be part of the qualitative data documented in diaries and protocols. On the other hand, potential subjectivity might be an unwelcomed intervening variable in quantitative research (Flick, 2014). Although involving different methodologies, either qualitative or quantitative approaches can be used in a longitudinal study.

Longitudinality: Contribution to Qualitative Methodology

Qualitative longitudinal research is distinct in the field of qualitative methodology and is widely recognized for its unique contributions (Thomson & McLeod, 2015). Characteristically, longitudinal studies involve a longer time span, enabling researchers to describe change. Thus, longitudinal research can be framed by time periods, stages, cycles, and phases (Saldaña, 2003). Most studies provide a snapshot describing a phenomenon at the time of the research (Flick, 2014), or examine a specific, present moment in a "one-off" design (McLeod & Thomson, 2011). Longitudinal methods, on the other hand, expand the qualitative perspective by enabling the researcher to examine processes over time or, as Flick (2014) observes, by allowing for a consistent and an ongoing approach to analyzing developments. Over time, change and the strategies used to manage that change are understood (Neale & Flowerdew, 2003). Thus, how people respond to change is relevant.

Replication studies are similar to longitudinal designs, but a replication study's goal is to determine if the same result is obtained through the same methods used in the original research. The medical field, for example, is well known for conducting replication studies. Researchers frequently repeat tests on a new drug to determine its medical results. In contrast, a qualitative longitudinal study's purpose is to track individuals or groups to investigate change over time. Using the medical example, if the purpose is to understand how individuals' emotional responses change over time with a drug's continued use, feelings are explored rather than the dispassionate drug test results. However, the long-term interaction between researcher and participants might probe uncomfortable feelings about an experience and, thus, make participants uneasy (McLeod & Thomson, 2011). Then later during member checking or in a publication although anonymized, one's thoughts and comments can potentially evoke both positive and negative emotions such as delight, surprise, and denial.

This book provides examples of qualitative methodologies, including grounded theory, ethnography, and case study. It also builds and expands on such methods as interviews, observations, and focus groups. Throughout this book, I assume that the reader is familiar with these methodologies and methods of qualitative research. This book's main purpose is to add the dimension of time and thus illustrate how the interaction of time and context in a longitudinal qualitative study leads to understanding and interpreting change as it unfolds.

THE VALUE OF QUALITATIVE LONGITUDINAL STUDIES

Researchers, policy makers, and leaders want to know the impact of an initiative or a program. Longitudinal qualitative studies provide a method of understanding such influence over time, whereas a short-term study focuses on a single point in time. In addition, qualitative longitudinal studies give researchers access to rich data sources for publishing multiple studies, which significantly contributes to a scholarship agenda.

Many Studies Resulting From One Data Set

A large volume of data is rich with possibilities for research and publication. Most studies have a limited focus, describing a phenomenon at the time of the research (Flick, 2014). Investigating a specific, present-moment issue is sometimes referred to as a "snapshot" or a "one-off design" (McLeod & Thomson, 2011). On the other hand, longitudinal methods enable researchers to examine processes over time, thus allowing ongoing analysis in multiple ways or views. Consequently, a single study can result in many publications. Table 1 illustrates the numerous studies published thus far using the same data set on teacher evaluation.

Longitudinal qualitative research is an appropriate methodology for evaluating implementation of specific policies and the strategies individuals use to manage that change over time (McLeod & Thomson, 2011; Neale & Flowerdew, 2003). For example, one of my goals in a 5-year study of 14 principals was to understand change in teacher policies and the strategies principals used to manage the policy implementation. Using a change theory as a theoretical frame, I reported how principals' perceptions of teacher evaluation changed during the implementation of a new teacher-evaluation mandate. As the change theory predicted, the initial year was characterized by frustration with time-management difficulties and expectations regarding the supervisory role (Derrington & Campbell, 2015). In the second and third years, following the theme of change, I analyzed the similarities and differences in responses from year to year. This study also illustrated changes in principals' perceptions during the implementation of a new teacher-evaluation system in Tennessee. Beginning in 2011, 14 principals participated in annual interviews through 2016. I asked the same 11 questions each year so that changes in principals' perceptions over time could be ascertained. To capture new developments, two or three new questions were added yearly to the repeated questions each year.

TABLE 1 ■ **Numerous Studies Using One Data Set**

Article	Journal or Book	Year
The changing conditions of instructional leadership: Principals' perceptions of teacher evaluation accountability mandates*	In B. G. Barnett, A. R. Shoho, & A. J. Bowers (Eds.), *International research on school leadership: Vol. 4. School and district leadership in an era of accountability* (pp. 231–251). Charlotte, NC: Information Age Publishing	2013
Metaphors and meaning: Principals' perception of teacher evaluation implementation	*Educational Leadership Review, 14*(3), 22–29	2013
Teacher evaluation initial policy implementation: Principals' and superintendents' perceptions	*Planning and Changing, 45*(1/2), 120–137	2014
Implementing new teacher evaluation systems: Principals' response to change and calls for support	*Journal of Educational Change, 16*(3), 305–326	2015
Principals' concerns and superintendent support during teacher evaluation changes	*AASA Journal of Scholarship and Practice, 12*(3), 11–22	2015
Implementing teacher evaluation: Lattice of leadership	*Journal of Research on Leadership Education, 11*(2), 181–199	2016
Teacher evaluation, formative supervision and instructional leadership	*UCEA Review*	2016
Implementing a new teacher evaluation system: Principal leadership and teacher job-embedded professional development**	*Professional Development in Education, 43*(4), 630–644	2016
Principals, policy, and practice: Supervision in the intersection	In S. Zepeda & J. Glanz (Eds.), *Re-examining supervision: Theory and practice*. Lanham, MD: Rowman & Littlefield, 129–143	2016

Article	Journal or Book	Year
Teacher Evaluation Policy Tools: Principals' Selective Use in instructional leadership*	*Leadership and Policy in Schools.* doi: 10.1080/15700763.2017.1326143	2017
School principals' views of teacher evaluation policy: Lessons learned from two empirical studies***	*International Journal of Leadership in Education, 20*(4), 416–431	2017
Principals as local actors in supervision	In S. Zepeda & J. Ponticell (Eds.), *Handbook of Educational Supervision.* Hoboken, NJ: Wiley-Blackwell	In Press

Note: *co-authored with J. W. Campbell; **with J. Kirk; ***with M. Flores

Because I asked the same questions each year, the 14 responses to each question could be examined collectively or one at a time. For example, respondents were asked to identify benefits of the new teacher-evaluation system. Interestingly, every year they identified the instructional rubric as the greatest benefit. Several questions focused on professional development, both offered and received. Over time, my analysis illustrated that leadership for professional development shifted from the district level to the schools. Because the principals came from four districts, the data was also examined by district. At the beginning of the study, I had planned to interview superintendents as another data source. However, I quickly recognized an opportunity for a new analysis comparing principals' and superintendents' perspectives of teacher-evaluation implementation (Derrington, 2014). The teacher perspective was added in yet another study. Teachers who worked with the participating principals were interviewed and surveyed to examine the nexus of principal and teacher perceptions of the teacher-evaluation implementation. Furthermore, many more studies are possible. For example, future studies might include a closer look at the 5-year data to determine if differences exist in principals' evaluation practices by grade level or by gender.

The Impact of Change

My epiphany about change began when I read the work of two "stage" theorists: Gale Sheehy, who wrote about adult life passages, and Elisabeth Kübler-Ross, who wrote about stages of grief. Although I had not yet

Advice for new assistant professors:

It's normal to have your study's end in mind but be cautious of only think-ing of the end. That's likely to result in a one-off study. Think of the entire process. Ask yourself what you might write about or study, for example describing the initiative, the beginning stages, and the processes used.

Dr. Jayson Richardson, Professor, San Diego State University

acquired research skills, I realized that individuals experience transitions involving change over time, thus leading to insights into themselves and others. That concept remained with me and became fundamental to my investigation of how policy plans and unexpected political events affect school leadership.

Hall and Hord's (2011) research-based observation about change is common sense but is still worth repeating: "Change is a process not an event" (p. 8). As these authors illustrated, change is not a one-time event such as issuing a state or district mandate. Instead, it occurs gradually over years and includes the learning process of individuals and organiza-tions as they adapt to change. The longer a researcher is involved with participants, the greater the insight (McLeod & Thomson, 2011). As I began my research, I understood the value of the long view and my tremendous opportunity to understand participants' perspectives and how those perspectives change over time.

Researchers in education as well as in other human services fields are interested in transforming the status quo by successfully implementing ini-tiatives and policies. Qualitative longitudinal methodology is essential for analyzing the implication of initiatives and policies over time. Moreover, this approach provides the most consistent way of analyzing developments and processes as they unfold continuously rather than examining the end point or outcome (Flick, 2014; McLeod & Thomson, 2011; Miller, 2015). In other words, single-implementation studies provide a snapshot of change, whereas longitudinal qualitative studies provide an album of change.

Studies examining the initial stage of change and implementation often magnify short-term failures and time-management issues. On the other hand, long-term studies assist in uncovering sustained changes and imple-mentation successes. Consequently, researchers seeking to understand a change's effect must do so over time. Participants during the first year of a change are frequently concerned with personal issues, such as managing time and materials (Hall & Hord, 2015). For example, not receiving new textbooks on time leads to frustration and to the uncertainty and insecurity of not meeting a supervisor's expectations. While attending an American Educational Research Association (AERA) conference, a colleague and I attended a session on the perspectives of principals as they adapted to a newly mandated statewide teacher-evaluation system. The presenter, new to research, briefly studied the implementation's initial stage and concluded that teacher evaluation frustrates and confuses principals. Contrast this snapshot view with a longitudinal view of a change in a teacher-evaluation system. A longitudinal study uncovers the change in the principals' perceptions and attitudes over time. The result of my 5-year study of principals' teacher-evaluation implementation revealed that principals' personal concerns dominated early in the implementation then lessened in subsequent years. I concluded that as familiarity deepens, principals begin focusing on larger effects, such as increased student learning, that might result from the new evaluation system (Derrington & Campbell, 2015). Researchers risk making inaccurate assumptions or generalizations when a brief period in a change process is studied. Inferences based on a snippet of time can cause a researcher to mistakenly conclude that less complex processes are profound.

THE CHALLENGES OF QUALITATIVE LONGITUDINAL STUDIES

In this section, the challenges of participant attrition and of time are discussed. Along with examples of each challenge are strategies for removing obstacles.

Participant Attrition

Participant attrition is a problem in any longitudinal study, whether qualitative or quantitative. The longer a study continues, the more likely unanticipated events might interfere with the research. Participants might exit an ongoing study for many reasons: retirement; changes in life or work circumstances; or a move to a new geographic location, resulting in not being able to be located because participants might not think of leaving a forwarding address with the researcher. Also, the smaller the sample, the more attrition negatively affects the outcome.

Any study benefits from careful planning; however, such planning can be especially crucial in longitudinal studies. Flick (2014) notes that identifying the processes for locating and following participants before beginning the study is imperative. Yet even careful planning does not guarantee locating all participants. Consider Galloway and Kapasi's study (2015), which surveyed 600 students who took a university-level entrepreneurship class, and then was followed up with another survey some years later. Attempting to ensure that students could be located later, the researchers considered steps. They requested university and personal e-mail addresses as well as home and mobile telephone numbers. However, only five participants were found through e-mails and phone numbers 7 years later. Continuing to search for the former students, Galloway and Kapasi then used Facebook and LinkedIn, technology unavailable for the original study. Some were found and contacted through social media, but the large number of people with the same name made narrowing the search difficult. Using the search method and eliminating from consideration those who chose not to participate in the study, Galloway and Kapasi had only 10 of the original 600 participants in the new study.

Despite attrition issues, a study need not perish as these authors illustrated. Study designs can be flexible to accommodate a longitudinal approach. Subsequently, Galloway and Kapasi (2015) conducted case studies involving the 10 subjects located, producing a valuable mixed-methods study with interesting results. They conducted one-to-one interviews, obtained background information and data on each participant, and triangulated this data with the original study's survey data. This example illustrates that even when a longitudinal study's possible participant attrition is meticulously planned, the unexpected can occur. However, resourceful researchers find ways to return to participants or sites over time (McLeod & Thomson, 2011). The research can continue if the researcher is ingenious and rethinks the study.

Another illustration of anticipating and handling attrition is seen in my 5-year study of the perceptions and experiences of principals as they implemented teacher evaluation. Each year changes occurred, most often through principals' transfers to other schools. As a result, 10 principals in the fifth year were the same with whom the study began. This attrition may not seem significant; but with only 14 principals in the study, any loss could affect the data's credibility. Early in designing the study, I made the fortuitous decision to keep schools in the study regardless of principal changes, thus allowing the context to remain the same and the data to be less confounded. Surprisingly, in all instances but one, when a principal left, an assistant principal ascended to the principal's position or a principal from another school in the same district assumed leadership of the school. Following this discovery, I pondered the significance of promoting an assistant principal rather than hiring from outside the school. I realized that this data might provide insight into principal succession in school districts.

Knowledge of the context, topic and participants assists the qualitative longitudinal researcher in anticipating unexpected events. For example, as both a principal and a superintendent, I had firsthand knowledge that leadership continually changes in many schools. Thus, anticipating this change, I planned to continue with the same schools regardless of principal changes. At the time, I did not realize the wisdom of that plan. I also planned to interview teachers. Working with the same schools allowed the context to remain constant. Moreover, I developed a relationship with the school secretary through ongoing communication. Then when a change in leadership occurred, I contacted this important gatekeeper to make an appointment with the new principal and remind the secretary of my study. I also included the principals' supervisor—the superintendent—in ongoing communication, indicating, for example, when I would be interviewing in the district or when a study had been published. Throughout the years and the changes, I found that a longitudinal qualitative researcher must not only maintain communications and relationships but also show appreciation, requirements more fully explored in Chapter 4. Additionally, frequent communication allows efficient and ongoing tracking of participants' changes, publication data needed for demographic tables.

The Issue of Time

Mentoring a beginning assistant tenure-track professor, I encouraged him to think of his scholarship agenda's longitudinality potential. He responded, "Sure, I can see the value, but longitudinal studies take a looooong time. And I don't have it if I'm expected to publish two or three articles a year." He had a legitimate concern if he wanted to remain employed. If asked how much time is needed for a longitudinal study, many researchers would probably respond, as my colleague did, that longitudinal studies take a long time and consequently are unrealistic for those under pressure to publish. However, time is elastic in a longitudinal study. According to Saldaña (2003), at least two data-collection points are necessary to be considered longitudinal: "the then and now" (p. 75). He added that additional points might be described as "then, and then, and then, and then, and now" (p. 76). Furthermore, the concept of time varies greatly in longitudinal studies depending on the research design. Considering the time involved in longitudinal studies, doctoral students and tenure-seeking assistant professors might believe such studies are unrealistic within their time constraints. In the following chapters, I challenge that notion by describing and illustrating ways that qualitative longitudinal studies can be designed within a timeframe.

Chapter Summary

Qualitative longitudinal studies offer a unique opportunity to understand change. Yes, there are challenges; but in my experience, those are easily overcome with persistence, flexibility, and a desire to dig deeply and understand. In summary, qualitative longitudinal studies

- provide a deeper understanding of an issue,
- allow significant interaction with participants,
- build on qualitative research skills, and
- can yield many studies from one data set.

Finally, although many qualitative longitudinal studies are well planned in advance a longitudinal study can emerge from unexpected opportunities and new insights as well. Keep longitudinality in mind as a way of expanding your study and of digging deeper into issues and changes.

Reflection Questions and Application Activities

- What information presented in this chapter connected to and extended your knowledge of qualitative longitudinal research?

- Describe how a program or policy might benefit from a qualitative longitudinal study of change.

- You are in the middle of a 5-year longitudinal qualitative research project. Every year, you hold semistructured interviews with the same 10 participants. Unfortunately, as you begin to schedule this year's interviews, you learn that two of your participants have dropped from the study: one relocated across the country, and the other no longer wished to be involved in the project. How would you manage this change and why would you choose that option?

How would you manage the identified challenges of conducting qualitative longitudinal studies?

DESIGNING QUALITATIVE LONGITUDINAL STUDIES

Qualitative research design basics are the foundation of the longitudinal qualitative study. However, some elements beyond the basic design must be considered.

In this chapter, the reader will

- review qualitative research design basics,
- learn to include longitudinality in a basic qualitative study design,
- consider stage theories as a useful way to describe and analyze change, and
- anticipate ethical issues prior to engaging in the Institutional Review Board (IRB) approval process.

DESIGN BASICS IN QUALITATIVE RESEARCH

Simply stated, a research design is a study's blueprint or plan. A comprehensive discussion of design's elements can be found in such well-known texts as John W. Creswell's *Research Design* and Uwe Flick's *An Introduction to Qualitative Research*. Both texts also include a checklist for determining if a design includes the necessary components. As an overview of a qualitative study's proposal, Creswell (2003) presents clear and useful proposal outlines. Although not all studies adhere to an exact format, a typical proposal for a doctoral dissertation includes the following elements:

Introduction

    Statement of the problem

    Purpose of the study

    Research questions or protocols*

    Theoretical perspective*

    Definition of terms

    Delimitations and limitations

Literature Review*

Methods

    Type of research design

    Sample population and participants

    Data-collection instruments, variables, and materials

    Data-analysis procedures**

Anticipated ethical issues *

Significance of the study

EXPANSION OF THE BASIC DESIGN

The basic design outlined in the previous section can be expanded to accommodate a longitudinal study by placing increased attention on the design sections indicated with an asterisk (*). This chapter explores longitudinal considerations in the literature review, a research study's protocols, theoretical frameworks, and ethical issues. Data analysis, indicated with a double asterisk (**), is the topic of Chapter 6.

Research Protocols

Developing a longitudinal study's protocol is similar to that of other qualitative research because the researcher chooses surveys, interviews, or other data-collection methods in the initial design. However, unlike the basic design, a longitudinal study builds on the frequency of data collection. The researcher determines how frequently and for how long data will be collected. After reading an early draft of this book, a student observed that frequency, or how often a measurement was taken, is quite variable in studies. He asked me how a researcher determines frequency of data collection points. One way is developing a rationale for frequency based on the researcher's underlying theory in the study (Bolger & Laurenceau, 2013). For example, Bolger and Laurenceau used quantitative measures to collect five pieces of data over a short time to assess goodness of fit. Applying this approach, I determined that 5 years was sufficient for identifying principals' perceptions of a new teacher-evaluation reform. I based this decision on implementation literature, which suggested that longitudinally investigating reform implementation might reveal differences unapparent in the initial implementation stage, thus indicating that the process of change is likely to span multiple years (Hall & Hord, 2015; Honig, 2006). Based on my experience and observations as a school administrator, many implementations plateau by the fifth year. Thus, I chose to conduct a 5-year study.

Saldaña (2003) describes frequency as waves of data collection, indicating regularity in data collection such as once a year across 5 years. The data collection's frequency and the study's time span can be determined in various ways. For example, the implementation of a program or change might have beginning, middle, and ending dates that become the data-collection points. Perhaps significant events might be anticipated that could create a logical timeline to collect perceptions. For ongoing data collection, the researcher might also consider key points of time such as transitions, changes, or stages. For example, when studying patient care, regularly occurring points in treatment can be identified and the changing opinions, perceptions, experiences, and needs can be assessed over time. At times, the researcher combines knowledge of the change with logic about the best time to collect data.

The following three examples of frequency and time frame provide additional considerations for determining important data-collection points in a longitudinal study.

Example one

Giaever and Smollan (2015) explored the complexity and dynamism of affective experiences during a public hospital's organizational change. The researchers interviewed 11 nurses at three points in time about a technological change: specifically, introduction of electronic care plans. Replacing pen and paper reports, this technology required structured computer-mediated summaries of patient problems. The researchers conducted interviews 1 month before implementation, as well as 3 months and 1 year after implementation. During the interviews, researchers asked participants to reflect forward and backward in time, describing emotional experiences regarding the organizational change. These researchers conjectured that changes in feelings during implementation would elicit different thoughts and behaviors. They displayed their findings in a chart comparing reported emotions at the three times data were collected. The longitudinal method was appropriate for looking more closely at the emotions of the nurses as they grappled with the organizational change's uncertainties and realities.

Example two

Okilwa and Barnett (2017) studied 20 years of sustained high academic performance in an elementary school. In the methodology section, they noted that four principals led school reforms from 1993 to 2014. Drawing on publications capturing the school's history and accomplishments, the researchers described the context over the years. In the section on data-collection instruments and procedures, they noted information was drawn from archival data and qualitative interviews conducted by the authors. Archival data included *Texas Academic Excellence From 1993–2011*, the US Department of Education report identifying the school as one of nine high-performing, high-poverty urban schools in Texas. After principals, teachers, and several parents were interviewed, the findings were described using Kotter's Change Frame, discussed later in this chapter.

Example three

In studying teacher evaluation, I considered the legislatively mandated annual evaluation process and timeline. Principals completed the first round of classroom observations and submitted written feedback by late fall. Therefore, I scheduled yearly principal interviews in December, a point in the annual cycle when principals would likely have completed the first round and would have sufficient experience to reflect on the evaluation process. Moreover, students' state test scores, a component of the new teacher-evaluation process, are typically available to schools in the early fall. Consequently, by December principals would have access to test data from the previous year as well as data obtained in the fall round of classroom observations. Although I considered conducting the interviews at the end of the school year, my experience with schools and my knowledge of spring events made me realize that principals would not welcome interviews at such a busy time nor would they have spring test data.

Each of these examples illustrates a linear data-collection design and a study that proceeds as anticipated. However, studies, like life, can throw curve balls. A research study's emergent nature requires flexibility (Saldaña, 2003). The unexpected can actually be advantageous by causing the researcher to rethink the design. For example, as thoroughly discussed in Chapter 1, when researchers Galloway and Kapasi (2015) located only a fraction of their original survey participants, they changed the design to include case studies of participants they did locate.

Theoretical Change Frameworks

"There is nothing more practical than a good theory." (Lewin, 1952, p. 169)

Although abstract, theories assist researchers in understanding experiences and relationships. I have come to appreciate that a good (i.e., useful) theory "gives you new insights and broadens your understanding of the phenomenon" (Anfara & Mertz, 2015, p. 5). When I was selected as a finalist for a tenure-track position at the University of Tennessee in Knoxville, I was invited for 2 days of both formal and informal interviews. I vividly recall a breakfast meeting in the Four Seasons hotel's café with Vincent Anfara, who was then the head of the Educational Leadership and Policy Studies Department. Between bites of breakfast, I explained my recent study, which used the grounded theory perspective developed during my doctoral work. Laying down his fork, he emphatically told me that being without a theory is impossible and that selecting a problem and creating research questions implied a perspective at work. I was taken aback by his strong feelings about using a theoretical framework and wondered how our research perspectives might clash if I were hired. Feeling my face redden, I considered excusing myself and packing my bag for a quick return to the Pacific Northwest. However, Dr. Anfara patiently outlined the benefits of a theoretical frame as a research study lens. In reflecting on my growth as a researcher since that breakfast meeting, I have learned to locate and apply many different theories to develop publication-worthy research.

My breakfast meeting incident also revealed the ongoing debate regarding a framework's usefulness for collecting and sorting data. Some scholars support the use of either a priori knowledge or a defined framework as a roadmap for data collection and analysis. Others favor a construct flowing only from the data and an analysis that is the product of a completely open mind (Kearney & Hyle, 2015). One purpose of frameworks is to provide "clarity in design, data collection, and analysis that is impossible to get in any other way" (Kearney & Hyle, 2015, p. 194). Another purpose is to explain and make sense of the data without being straitjacketed, limiting analysis (Mills & Bettis, 2015). Regardless of the position on a theoretical frame's purpose, the researcher must carefully consider the effect of personal beliefs and experiences that constrain or skew a study's perspective.

Theoretical frameworks are frequently described as lenses through which to study phenomena. Frameworks are useful in many different fields including sociology, political science, psychology, and economics (Anfara & Mertz, 2015). According to Mills and Bettis (2015), a theoretical frame's purpose is to make sense of the data and to "move the research project beyond the realm of the descriptive into the realm of the explanatory" (p. 112). This view of theoretical frameworks applies to any qualitative study. However, a longitudinal study generates an abundance of data, potentially leading to using many theoretical frames. According to Anfara and Mertz (2015), "It is, indeed, this diversity and richness of theoretical frameworks that allow us to see in new and different ways what seems to be ordinary and familiar" (p. 15). I have also come to appreciate that while theory is a lens shaping multiple study design elements, in a qualitative longitudinal study, a theory can also provide a cohesive perspective of a phenomenon spanning multiple years by use of stage theories. Over time, multiple stages' progression may become evident. In the next section, I describe stage theories that have been effectively used in qualitative longitudinal studies to provide a cohesive perspective of change over multiple data collection points.

Stage Theories Useful for Describing Change

The many stage theories offer a starting point for considering a longitudinal study's framework. Discovering potential stage theories requires reading broadly in many social science fields, reflecting deeply on a model's adequacy to support the research envisioned, and searching the library in person or using electronic data bases to look beyond the obvious. Stages can be used for sorting rather than having to generate categories and themes emerging from data. From experience, I have learned that the large volume of data in a longitudinal study benefits from the organization a theoretical frame provides, particularly a stage model if it fits the study.

As a caveat, this discussion is a starting point for anyone undertaking longitudinal studies. The use of stages might appear to be an overly linear or rigid method of data collection and analysis. As Knapp (2017) observes, the research process is iterative, and the theoretic framework might be a starting point that can change and develop as the study unfolds. In addition, Saldaña (2003) warns that observing change is not guaranteed and that researcher bias or expectation should not be allowed to distort data.

Although the possibilities are numerous, an overview of five well-known models is presented below followed by a discussion of one of these model's application in a longitudinal study.

Hall and Hord's Concerns-Based Adoption Model

Hall and Hord's model addresses the affective side of change. Individuals typically progress through the following stages: need for information, personal, management of change, tasks, consequences, collaboration, and refocusing.

Kotter's Change Theory

Kotter (1995, 2012) developed an eight-step process considered essential to successful organizational change: (1) establishing a sense of urgency; (2) forming a powerful guiding coalition; (3) creating a vision; (4) communicating the vision; (5) empowering others to act on the vision; (6) planning for and creating short-term wins; (7) consolidating improvements, institutionalizing new approaches.

Kohlberg's Developmental Stage Model

According to Kohlberg's model, the basis of ethical behavior—moral reasoning—consists of six developmental stages: (1) obedience, (2) self-interest, (3) conformity, (4) authority, (5) social contract, and (6) universal principles. In each progressive stage, the individual becomes more competent at responding to moral dilemmas.

Erikson's Stages of Psychosocial Development

Erikson's model involves eight stages that a healthy, developing person should pass through from infancy to adulthood. During each stage, the person experiences a psychosocial crisis involving the psychological needs of the individual conflicting with the needs of society. Successful crisis resolution results in acquisition of eight basic virtues or character strengths: hope, will, purpose, competency, fidelity, love, care, and wisdom.

Kübler-Ross's Stages of Grief

Elisabeth Kübler-Ross's model was built on the belief that individuals experience five stages of grief: denial, anger, bargaining, depression, and acceptance.

Example Using the Kübler-Ross Framework. Most of us spend much of our day working in organizations: hospitals, schools, businesses, or nonprofits. In addition to earning a salary, we develop friendships, gain skills, and become part of a routine pattern of service or production. The introduction of an organizational change, although possibly for the better in the long term, frequently disrupts a familiar routine in the short term. Consequently, organizational change's long-term impact can be understood using a theoretical frame as part of a longitudinal research design. In a study of organizational change, Kearney and Hyle (2015) applied Kübler-Ross's grief model to examine imposed organizational changes' emotional impact on individuals. As a senior corporate trainer in 1999 at WorldCom, during a merger with MCI, Kearney struggled to find a way to manage the massive change. She realized that individuals were grieving and that emotions were a major factor in the change. When she left to pursue her doctorate, she met faculty member Hyle. The two had a similar interest in organizational change and began a long-term collaboration. They speculated that lack of attention to individuals and their emotional experiences during change leads to failure. Searching for organizational change frameworks, they reviewed a wide variety of grief constructs before identifying Kübler-Ross's model as the most appropriate for several reasons. It was (1) well researched and accepted as a model, (2) practical to use as a data-collection tool and as an analysis instrument, (3) easy to understand and visualize, and (4) appropriate for examining change's emotional impact on individuals. They also coded interview transcripts using this model. The researchers focused on a school when the superintendent changed. The former superintendent had been in the district 17 years, a long time for someone in that position. Although from the area, the new superintendent had a different philosophy, creating changes for the school's employees. For example, he created a technology school, training high school students to obtain their certifications and licensures.

Using Multiple Frames

More than one theoretical framework might apply to the same data set. For example, Mills and Bettis (2015) and their colleagues examined a college of education as it reorganized its departmental structure. During the yearlong reorganization, they systematically journaled their experiences, feelings, and reactions. Journal entries from five participants were subsequently coded and analyzed with themes applied based on the chosen theoretical frames. The researchers considered frameworks from leadership, organizational change, and organizational culture. All might have worked, but ultimately, they settled on organizational identity and liminality. In making the choice a factor was the unit of analysis to be studied (i.e., individuals—not a department or college). Studying individuals led to frameworks other than leadership or organization. Another factor was the researchers' familiarity with and understanding of a specific theory. Mills's doctoral program and subsequent teaching in higher education centered on organizational identity. Bettis's study of liminality, the transition period between stages, also began with her doctoral work. The following titles of the two studies and the publishing journals indicate the versatility and breath possible through the lens of various frameworks applied to the same longitudinal data set.

Bettis, P. J., Mills, M., Miller, J., & Nolan, R. (2005). Faculty in a liminal landscape. A case study of college reorganization. *Journal of Leadership and Organizational Studies, 11*(3), 47–61.

Mills, M., Bettis, P. J. Miller, J., & Nolan, R. (2005). Experiences of academic unit reorganization: Organizational identity and identification in organizational change. *Review of Higher Education, 28*(4), 597–619.

Literature Review

A longitudinal study's initial literature review is similar to that of any qualitative study. A key difference, however, is that because of a longitudinal study's longer duration, new information and other studies on the topic will inevitably be published as the study unfolds. Consequently, a researcher must continually scan the literature for new information to keep the literature review current. Many notification services are available to alert researchers to recently published information on topics. I subscribe to several notification services, such as SAGE Publishing, to receive alerts on teacher evaluation. Such services allow subscribers to designate topics and frequency of alerts. For example, go to https://us.sagepub.com/en-us/nam/researchers-emai-alerts. From this page, an account is created and choices are made under Journal Content Alerts journal choices to receive alerts and updated announcements.

Anticipation of Ethical Issues

This section highlights the importance of anticipating and addressing potential ethical issues early in designing a longitudinal qualitative study. Various ethical issues are examined in Chapter 4. Qualitative research is characterized by open-endedness and intimacy, thus making it more likely to come under the scrutiny of the Institutional Review Board (IRB) (Howe & Dougherty, 1993). Howe and Dougherty (1993) emphasize that using the term *participants*, rather than *subjects* as in traditional studies, implies a closer relationship as does the face-to-face interviews and observations necessary in a qualitative method. This familiarity between researchers and participants is compounded by extended contact in a longitudinal study. In addition, a qualitative study unfolds and develops as meaning is created, thus complicating fully informed consent before the research begins. As a result, benefits and risks might be difficult to determine in advance as the interview term *open-ended* questioning implies; thus, the term will likely attract the IRB's attention. Agreeing that some issues such as informed consent and the right to privacy must be considered in advance, Merriam and Tisdell (2016) view other issues arising in the field as being resolvable as they appear. They believe that preestablished general guidelines give way to the investigator's own sensitivity and values. Qualitative methods continue to evolve; and as acceptance of the methodology increases, the IRB may be more accepting of some flexibility. The IRB was created to protect research participants' rights by closely scrutinizing ethical issues arising in a study. Thus, thinking through and addressing these potential hazards in advance can save weeks resubmitting a proposal after the IRB review. The IRB must be informed of all study-related procedures, including any expectations the researcher has regarding follow-up protocols. Across all the University of Tennessee's colleges, the top reasons for IRB proposal rejection are based on ethical issues (Institutional Review Board, University of Tennessee. February 2017 *HRPP Newsletter,* Volume 3, Issue I).

The following are commonly used procedures that are frequently not mentioned in the IRB application but that are discovered later:

- recordings and any type of recordings, e.g., audio and visual that will be used

- collecting, obtaining, or reviewing existing records or other data. When used for research, the data must be identified. Such data can include datasets, course assignments, and artifacts. In the case of datasets, each data point to be obtained/reviewed/abstracted must be identified.

- follow-up interviews or data collections

- returning transcripts to research participants to review for accuracy and feedback

- identifying all data-collection instruments to be used including requests for demographic information

Chapter Summary

This chapter has examined how designing a longitudinal study expands on the design of a one-point-in-time study. Like the Global Positioning System (GPS) in a car, when a recalculation occurs, a study's directional change leads to arriving at the intended research destination. The following points must be considered when planning the route a study will follow:

- Stay current on the literature related to your topic throughout the research by subscribing to journal e-mail alerts as new articles will be published throughout a longitudinal study's duration.

- Determine the frequency of data collection based on your knowledge of the field, the topic, the implementation steps' significance, and the research question.

- Explore various fields and disciplines for appropriate stage theories useful for describing change over time.

- Anticipate ethical concerns inherent in qualitative methods, especially in longitudinal studies requiring long-term contact with participants. Address those concerns while developing your IRB proposal.

Reflection Questions and Application Activities

- How can you apply the information in this chapter to a study you are considering?

- Locate a qualitative longitudinal study in your discipline. Analyze how the author described and used a theoretical framework.

- What are the benefits and drawbacks of using a change stage theory in a qualitative longitudinal study?

BUILDING ON QUALITATIVE RESEARCH WITH A LONGITUDINAL DESIGN

In this chapter, the reader will

- explore qualitative longitudinal studies applied to various methodologies,

- examine examples of qualitative studies using a longitudinal approach, and

- consider longitudinal studies' importance in understanding change.

L ongitudinal qualitative research is not limited to certain fields and disciplines. Although qualitative research originated in anthropology and sociology, it is used internationally in education as well as various other social sciences, including such fields as child development, life history, and organizational research. Searching the university library system for longitudinal studies, I found 1,806,790 sources covering a wide range of topics, such as supportive parenting, entrepreneurial small firms, and nurses' experience in restructuring organizations.

My search in the *International Journal of Qualitative Research* yielded an additional 335,832 studies. Furthermore, longitudinal qualitative research designs can encompass a range of methodologies (Thomson & McLeod, 2015). The following discussion provides examples of how various qualitative longitudinal methodologies are applied. Regardless of the chosen methodology, longitudinal studies examine change over time. As the following examples illustrate, a researcher can approach a study using a wide variety of methodologies.

HISTORICAL STUDIES

As part of my doctoral research requirement at the University of Washington, Seattle, I somewhat reluctantly enrolled in a historical research methodology course. At the time, I viewed historical research as the domain of dowdy archivists with dusty books and curious objects. I took the class because it fit into my schedule and the professor teaching it had a reputation for being humorous and for making research come alive. Surprisingly, I learned that history is more than storytelling or stringing together facts. Instead, it is a way to capture ideas and events and then interpret and communicate them (Johnson & Christensen, 2014). I eventually combined case studies with my interest in the history of people and policy into a dissertation research topic investigating the school principal's evolutionary leadership role.

Historical perspectives imply longitudinal development as the researcher reconstructs events and the actions of individuals or groups leading to those events (Burgleman, 2011). This type of research can also be described as a looking-backward approach, retracing time and seeking significant changes and critical events (Burgleman, 2011). For example, in a chapter titled "The Principal: Building the Future Based on the Past" (Derrington, in press), I discuss the historical evolution of principals' supervisory responsibilities in the context of national policies as principals implemented those policies in practice. The chapter chronicles the key models of teacher supervision aligned with significant federal policies and describes how federal policies and supervision models have evolved simultaneously. When working on this study, I found that some historical material is available online but that many older books are out of print and unavailable. Thus, a comprehensive investigation likely requires searching the library's shelves for primary resources.

Another example of looking-backward historical research involves using social media (Robards & Lincoln, 2017). Scrolling back through 5 years of Facebook accounts of 34 individuals in their twenties, Robards and Lincoln identified how stories of growing up were told using Facebook timelines. During interviews, the participants acted as co-analysts with the researcher in analyzing and discussing timeline posts. The scroll-backward method allowed researchers to understand how participants' social media disclosures changed over time. Viewing Facebook as a memory archive, the authors found complex life narratives. It appears social media has just begun to be an effective longitudinal research tool. These examples illustrate that events can be retraced with a goal of identifying, describing, and analyzing change.

Historical research can also incorporate a forward-looking approach allowing a researcher to theorize what might occur. For example, looking forward in an article on history of principals' supervisory responsibilities, I used a model of change, theorizing how policy and practice relate to teacher evaluation within the context of supervision and policymaking. I described future implications and possible outcomes for educational supervision given the federal policy's direction. The implication is that teacher supervision will continue to evolve as new political leaders emerge and federal mandates change. In fact, the next supervision model may be right around the next election corner.

TREND STUDIES

Participants' perspectives over time can reveal trends different from a one-point-in-time study. Trend studies examine groups of different people over time using the same questions (Johnson & Christensen, 2014) as well as additional data. As illustrated in the following examples, trend studies are appropriate for examining change at the group, not the individual, level (Taris, 2000).

A colleague and I conducted a descriptive study in 1993 to examine change in female superintendents' perceptions over time and to assess data trends. We designed a survey based on the literature that indicated a woefully low number of female superintendents. Then we surveyed aspiring female superintendents who were members of the Washington Association of School Administrators (WASA) and reported their perception of barriers to and support in achieving this leadership position (Sharratt & Derrington, 1993). Thirteen years later, data indicated that the number of female superintendents had not increased substantially. Thus, we wondered if the perceptions of aspiring females had changed regarding barriers thwarting their ascendency. We sent the same survey to women on the WASA list serve. Comparing their perceptions—the "then and now" (Saldaña, 2003, p. 75), we published the results (Derrington & Sharratt, 2009a; Derrington & Sharratt, 2009b). I believed our publications were the end of the study when I left Washington State for the University of Tennessee. Surprisingly, two Washington State professors, also former superintendents, contacted me in 2015 to followup on the study. They understood that change in women's career opportunities must be examined longitudinally and that using the same questions and procedures would facilitate this look across time. It is exciting to have 23 years and three data points to report on the progress (or lack thereof) that Washington State women have made in breaking barriers when aspiring to be superintendents (Hill, McDonald, Derrington, & Calderone, 2017).

Another trend study examining changes in group behaviors and perceptions over time focused on how school superintendents were leading districts in school improvement using technology. After completing a study, Richardson (2018) realized that technology use had exploded over 15 years. Thus, he wanted to determine if superintendents' technology leadership had also changed. Richardson identified tech-savvy superintendents by compiling names of the Tech-Savvy Superintendent Award recipients from the *eSchoolNews* web site. Honoring individuals at the forefront of technological understanding, this award acknowledges them as national models for other superintendents. According to his interview protocol, Richardson posed the same 14 questions to both groups. As seen in previous longitudinal studies, each question could become the foundation for a publication. For example, Richardson asked if superintendent preparation or administrative licensure programs assisted in developing technology skills. Based on that data, a publication might discuss preparation curriculum for tech-savvy school leaders. As another example, two interview questions focused on professional development opportunities focusing on technology skill-building and, in turn, the skills principals and teachers are provided. The Richardson study also illustrates that finding participants can be challenging. Searching the Internet (including such social networking sites as LinkedIn, Twitter, and Facebook) to locate past award recipients, he found the e-mail addresses and/or telephone numbers for 59 of 100 recipients from 2001 to 2010 and 32 of the 37 award recipients from 2011 to 2014. As in any longitudinal study, planning for attrition is imperative, especially the further back in time the researcher explores.

Trend studies involve research conducted at two or more times on two or more cross-sectional studies of different participants (Taris, 2000). In this approach, the samples are comparable (e.g., members of the same organization or children of the same age). Furthermore, the same surveys are used so the data can be compared across time. A trend study allowed Dr. Richardson to see how the field of educational technology matured and is evolving. Rather than examining one person or one school, he studied school leadership views of the field of technology.

ETHNOGRAPHY

Derived from anthropology, *ethnography* is the study of people interacting in a group. This interaction over time evolves into a culture or the patterns of behavior and beliefs for how people do things in that culture (Patton, 2002). Ethnography involves the application of a cultural perspective to explain findings, thus making it appealing and relevant in organizational studies. Ethnographic techniques have been applied to a variety of societal and social problems. Sometimes described as a translator of culture, the ethnographic researcher "works to understand another's world and then to translate the text of lived actions into a meaningful account" (Glesne, 2016, p. 224). The researcher is a meaning-maker or sense-maker of the events and situations experienced and explored during sustained fieldwork. During an ethnographic study, the researcher is immersed in the field, typically in participant observation while gathering data frequently daily or weekly across extended time periods.

Understanding the achievement challenges facing urban secondary schools has recently been a significant research topic resulting from numerous policy-reform initiatives. Stich and Cippolone (2017) used a longitudinal ethnographic methodology to study low-performing urban secondary schools. This study was part of a larger two-state study. The researchers followed groups of selected students over three years from early high school to graduation. They conducted interviews, observed classrooms, attended meetings, and visited students' homes. The duration of the study and the depth of data collection yielded findings and insights not possible in a one-time study. These researchers noted that the passage of time was important in understanding a context experiencing rapid change. Because of continuous change, the effects of an initiative or a reform might appear very different from one moment to the next. As the authors noted in a 2018 interview, the longitudinal ethnographic research moves beyond short-sighted, static representations of everyday life and has the potential for building deeper relationships with participants.

RESEARCHER ADVICE

"We advise someone embarking on a study of this kind to understand the costs and demands of this kind of work, but not be dissuaded from utilizing a longitudinal approach. Ultimately, because of the power of this approach, we feel it is worth the investment."

Stich and Cippolone, 2018 interview

AUTOETHNOGRAPHY

Autoethnography focuses on one's culture and oneself by using personal experiences to develop insights into one's larger culture or subculture. Like the other research approaches discussed, autoethnography can span a length of time, thus adding longitudinality. However, autoethnography poses many challenges, such as the researcher's need to balance the autobiographical perspective with the cultural context (Winkler, 2017). According to Winkler, autoethnographers can become narcissistic and self-indulgent when they emphasize the autobiographical too much. However, she adds that if emphasis on the self is insufficient, then the study might be indistinguishable from ethnography. Winkler sought to illuminate micro-processes and dynamics of identity work in an academic working context. She adopted an analytic autoethnographic approach examining recalled experiences of her current employment in a university department. Focusing on four workday events, she demonstrated how they served as moments of identity work in the sense that they called for engaging in answering the question of who one is and how one should act. I advise reading Winkler's and other scholars' publications to gain a better understanding of this methodology. In addition, although most autoethnographic research has been conducted and reported by a solo researcher, autoethnographical studies conducted by multiple authors are emerging. According to Winkler, this collaborative approach has an increasing number of proponents.

GROUNDED THEORY

Grounded theory generates theory by searching for themes and patterns in the data using the constant comparative method and testing emergent concepts through additional fieldwork (Glesne, 2016; Patton, 2002).

Employing grounded theory in a longitudinal qualitative study, Gray and Smith (2000) sought to discover mentorship's effect(s) on student nurses following the introduction of an educational program leading to a diploma of higher education in nursing in the United Kingdom. The nursing cohort consisted of 10 students from a large Scottish college of nursing and midwifery who were interviewed five times during their 3-year coursework. Students also kept a diary to record their thoughts and experiences regarding mentorship during their practice placements. In addition, another seven students volunteered to participate by only keeping a diary. With the aid of Non-numerical Unstructured Data Indexing, Searching and Theorizing (NUD.IST),, data were analyzed using the constant comparative method. Findings indicate that diploma students quickly lose their idealistic view of their mentors and, over time, develop insight into the qualities required of an effective mentor. Students quickly become aware of the importance of choosing good role models and of learning their mentor's likes and dislikes, which influence their assessment's outcome. As students gain confidence and skills, a gradual distancing from their mentors is evident. Although Gray and Smith did a short-term study interviewing mentors and mentees, the addition of longitudinality made it possible to see over time students' changing perspective of effective mentors.

CASE STUDIES

Longitudinal case studies provide important insight on change. Case studies explore a specific program, event, or process to understand a larger phenomenon (Creswell, 2003; Rossman & Rallis, 2017). Data gathering involves numerous methods including observations, interviews, and document collection (Glesne, 2016). Adding longitudinality in a 3-year case study, Peck and Reitzug (2017) examined a persistently low-performing urban elementary school that became the focus of a state-mandated turnaround. A turnaround school's policy goal is to rapidly increase student performance with significant interventions such as principal replacement, staff replacement, and school closure. Such interventions can be disruptive, thus Peck and Reitzug (2017) investigated how educators at a turnaround school engaged with and reacted to parents, families, community-based organizations, and the surrounding area. During the 3 years, these researchers conducted 78 interviews, learned about the school through researching old newspaper articles and other artifacts, made approximately 30 site visits, and photographed the school community. At intermediate steps to initially make sense of the accumulating data set, they presented interim findings at conferences soliciting feedback to refine their emergent findings. Following coding and memo writing, they distilled findings and represented them thematically. Using a longitudinal approach, the researchers found that as in short-term or one-off studies, academic increases did not occur quickly. However, success was evident over time in other important dimensions such as parental involvement and increased positive relationships with community organizations. The longitudinal view provided a deeper examination and a more insightful view of change than a less time-intensive method would have allowed.

COMBINED METHODOLOGIES AND METHODS

Using a combination of research designs (Flick, 2014), such as a historical comparative longitudinal study, is not unusual. However, the more complex a study becomes, the more closely a researcher must consider certain factors, such as research questions and time constraints. For example, consider a longitudinal comparative case study. In comparative case studies, situations or individuals are examined side-by-side to explore a dimension or phenomenon based on the research question. Thus, the goal is to examine cases in terms of a particular factor, not to observe entire cases in their complexity (Flick, 2014). Adding the longitudinal historical factor, a researcher might use case studies to examine the complexity of people, events, and changes.

Some examples in this chapter illustrate a combination of methodologies and methods. The use of a mixed methods design in longitudinal research is evolving as new understandings of the methodology develop (Creswell, 2003). Understandably, mixed methods are complex requiring research skills in more than one methodology, two or more data collection methods, and multiple points of time measurements. The few examples of mixed-method longitudinal studies found in the literature typically involve a survey followed by individual interviews with selected survey respondents. In the following example, I illustrate how one researcher used this mixed method design and added trend analysis as the longitudinal dimension.

David wanted to investigate how or if principals' perceptions of tenure's impact changed after the implementation of Tennessee legislation linking student test scores to teacher promotion and retention. He located a survey conducted 15 years before the new legislation. The earlier study's researcher distributed the survey to Tennessee teachers working at that time. After reviewing, updating, and piloting a slightly modified version of the survey, David distributed it electronically to all current Tennessee principals. He also wished to understand principals' beliefs about tenure in more depth than numbers alone would provide. At the survey's conclusion, principals could volunteer to participate in a phone interview for the study's qualitative portion. This interview's goals were to achieve a more comprehensive understanding of principals' perceptions of teacher tenure, to provide a means for increasing the findings' trustworthiness when data were analyzed and compared, and to adhere to parallel sampling techniques and recommendations within a mixed-methods design. He compared the 2016 principals' perceptions with those of the 1998 principals using the survey questions previously used (Lomascolo, 2016). In the final analysis, the most challenging aspect of this study was to integrate longitudinality and the results of both surveys and interviews.

David Lomascolo offered the following tips for designing a longitudinal study:

- When data sets are compared across or between periods of time, data-collection procedures should be mimicked as closely as possible.

- If the same participants are not in both studies, participants must be selected from the same context or geographic region.

- Mixed methods inform each component (i.e., the qualitative data-collection procedures expand the quantitative sample). The theoretical framework can serve as a link to integrate the two methodologies' findings.

Mixing Qualitative and Quantitative Data

Clear rules are not available for determining use of numbers in qualitative research. However, the argument is not if it should be done but for what purpose quantities are included (Miles & Huberman, 1994). Adding a quantitative component is done when it can provide richer detail in the study. As seen in examples, numbers can assist in trend analysis by revealing frequencies, thus providing a starting point to begin a deeper examination. Particularly in longitudinal qualitative research, numbers are useful to quickly see distributions and patterns within the large quantity of data (Miles & Huberman, 1994).

Use of Focus Groups

Focus groups are useful for more than data collection in a longitudinal research study. In addition to collecting data on a specific topic or issue, focus groups can be used to pilot a research instrument, refine research questions, and assist in research design and data collection strategies (Glesne, 2016).

Focus groups are small groups, typically five to eight people of similar backgrounds and experiences, brought together to participate in a group interview about issues affecting them. The terms *focus groups* and *group interviews* are not always used synonymously in the literature. A focus group often involves a fluid discussion so that multiple perspectives can be obtained while a group interview asks the same questions with participants taking turns answering. In the interview guide approach, Patton (2002) suggests creating an outline of topics or issues to be covered, thus systematically ensuring data collection's comprehensiveness.

A focus group can be combined with other methods or be used to clarify research findings gathered, making the focus group particularly useful in a longitudinal study. For example, after concluding a 5-year longitudinal study of principals' perceptions of teacher evaluation implementation, I developed a survey to examine teachers' perspectives of the findings. After analyzing the survey data, I moderated a focus group comprised of the principals in the original study to interview them regarding their interpretations of the combined principal and teacher data. Recording data from groups is challenging, even with a recorded transcript, because conversations overlap. I invited a graduate student and a colleague to take notes. A focus group's moderator is important to establish ground rules, keep track of time, and manage conversations so that every participant speaks. Group data collection saves time and travel; however, group interviews can inhibit confidentiality and make probing individual responses difficult (Glesne, 2016).

New technologies present interesting alternatives to the traditional face-to-face group data collection. Glesne (2016) suggests several methods, including an online focus group in real time with all participants simultaneously. The researcher poses a question and participants type responses transmitted to the entire group. Online forums can be recorded and are inexpensive and easy to schedule. Virtual reality is another possibility with participants using avatars in a real-time discussion. Non-real-time, or asynchronous, groups are also a possibility (e.g., e-mailing or posting questions to Blackboard or Canvas as frequently done in online courses). Yet another possibility is a blog for posing questions and collecting responses. However, when I experimented with collecting responses in an online course, this approach was difficult to facilitate and yielded less insight than in a face-to-face setting. Other challenges became apparent, such as the technological competence required when simultaneously managing the data collection technology and facilitating the dialogue. Upon reflection, I believe that technology presents new opportunities for data collection in focus groups and group interview approaches if the researcher is sufficiently proficient in combining technological expertise with solid research skills.

Chapter Summary

A wide range of methodologies can be used in longitudinal qualitative studies as the researcher seeks to understand how people make meaning and sense of experiences. The value in adding a longitudinal view is that the researcher develops a deeper insight on change than is likely to come from a one-point-in-time study. However, specific considerations are involved in each inquiry method. For example, ethnography's goal is to understand individuals' interaction with culture while grounded theory aims to build a theory about a phenomenon (Merriam, 2009). The qualitative longitudinal researcher must know the methodology and how to incorporate longitudinality as well. A challenging endeavor is likely to result in deep understanding of change.

Reflection Questions and Application Activities

- In your own words, explain how qualitative longitudinal studies differ from a one-point-in-time qualitative study.

- What idea in this chapter extended or pushed your thinking in a new direction?

- You are the director of institutional research and assessment at Magnificent University. Your boss, MU's president, has asked that your staff examine the long-term effects of a recently implemented policy limiting the number of on-campus extracurricular activities in which undergraduate students may participate. Your staff is already collecting longitudinal quantitative data. How might you collect and use longitudinal qualitative data? Which participants might you include in your assessment?

PERSPECTIVES ON THE TWO-WAY RESEARCH RELATIONSHIP

In this chapter, the reader will

- consider aspects of the personal and professional sides of a relationship with participants,

- understand ways to give back to research participants,

- learn ways to process ethical dilemmas, and

- add exit interviews and closure at a study's end.

This chapter explores the research relationship's benefits from both the researcher's and participants' viewpoints. In addition, ethical considerations related to the research relationship in a qualitative longitudinal study are discussed.

BALANCING PERSONAL AND PROFESSIONAL RELATIONSHIPS WITH PARTICIPANTS

Publish or perish! The only good dissertation is a done dissertation! These familiar expressions might lead one to be overly task oriented in conducting research. Researchers may struggle to balance their goals while meeting participants' need to be respected contributors to the research. Understandably, new professors are concerned with tenure and promotion. Equally clear is that the doctoral student's aspiration is not to stay in ABD status for eternity. However, objectifying or using participants to achieve one's personal career goals is repugnant to the ethical researcher. On the other hand, researchers might succumb to an overly friendly relationship with participants. For example, sometimes at final defenses, I ask doctoral candidates to discuss the most rewarding learning stage in his or her research and writing. Frequently and without hesitation, the candidate enthusiastically states that talking with participants was the most meaningful part of the experience. While this statement alone is not a concern, it is questionable when the candidate continues describing how conversations became exchanges of ideas with job-alike peers, drifting far from the intended data-collection interview questions. In the past, researchers were warned that forming friendships with participants might bias data collection and analysis. In the literature, terms for such involvement include *over identification* and *going native*. Glesne (2016), however, believes that friendships in the field today are not as inhibited as in the past. Nevertheless, such relationships should be respectful; reciprocal; and when possible, professionally trusting—not a close personal association characteristic of relationships with friends. For example, I often know the principals in my studies because we frequently attend the same professional meetings and share many of the same philosophies. However, I do not select them because they are friends, nor do I seek to develop closer bonds with them as I conduct studies.

These issues might apply to any qualitative research, but a longitudinal qualitative study's intensity and duration magnify them. In summary, the longitudinal qualitative researcher must balance the goal of completing a study with the researcher–participant trust relationship characteristic of qualitative research.

GIVING BACK TO PARTICIPANTS

Reciprocity is a two-way street, recognizing the researcher's and the participants' mutual benefits (Rossman & Rallis, 2012). Longitudinal qualitative research requires much of participants, who give time, share thoughts and stories, and yet can receive little in return. In fact, Glesne (2016) suggests that the closer the relationship, the greater the possibilities for reciprocation. The researcher must be cognizant of what participants wish to gain from the interaction, making participation worthwhile. Possibilities for researcher reciprocation include communicating throughout a study and giving appropriate tokens of appreciation.

Giving Appropriate Tokens of Appreciation

The researcher might also consider small tokens of appreciation to participants for their time. Greeting cards for holidays and birthdays are an inexpensive way to show appreciation (McLeod & Thomson, 2011). Also, thank-you notes are always appropriate. In recognizing qualitative research participants, reciprocity rarely involves monetary gifts; nevertheless, there are other ways to thank people for their time and involvement. Glesne (2016) suggests providing interviewees snacks or coffee. In an interview, Okilwa and Barnett (2017) discussed being mindful of scheduling interviews at a time convenient for participants; if that was lunch time, they brought lunch. According to Okilwa and Barnett, feeding the participants lunch created a more relaxed environment. These researchers also believe that going the extra mile conveyed the study's importance and the researchers' willingness to do whatever was necessary to gather the information.

The amount invested in thanking participants should be proportional to the time they invest and their level of involvement in the topic. For example, a yearly interview asking for perceptions of a workplace innovation likely requires less involvement than a study following individuals throughout a life transition. After each yearly interview, I sent a thank-you note to the interviewees in the 5-year study. Then after the fifth year, I applied for and received a $200 university grant to purchase thank-you gift baskets containing a coffee mug, candy, and a gift card to a local store. I delivered this more substantial gift at the study's conclusion to long-term involvement.

Communicating and Sharing Research Results

While at an American Education Research Association conference, I attended a presentation by Dr. Jason Richardson, associate professor at San Diego State, on a longitudinal study he conducted. Interested in his perspectives on the research relationship, I followed up with a phone interview. Dr. Richardson offered the following advice for conducting a longitudinal study:

> Build a relationship and continue to talk with these folks [the participants]. We do them a huge disservice if we don't give them something back. Much more is required than sending out an email like is done in a one-off [study].

When I asked him how he built rapport with participants, he responded,

Ask yourself what's in it for them? Give them something back. This aspect is not as big a repercussion in a one-off study, but it is important in a longitudinal study. Lots of researchers don't think to give back. You can give them professional development on the findings and results and work with the faculty. So, then the results are more meaningful in their eyes.

As a benefit of involvement, participants might gain insight into their experience. Okilwa and Barnett studied principals who led a school that against the odds achieved at a high level for over 20 years. These principals asked to participate in the study and reflect on and share their leadership experiences at the school many years prior. One principal noted, "I wasn't too sure about doing this at first. But I appreciated being able to think through what happened at that time."

Participants typically are interested in a study's findings and eager to read results. In addition to sharing research findings, treating interviewees with respect and listening carefully are ways to reciprocate (Glesne, 2016).

Allowing Participants to Be Heard

The interview is an opportunity for reciprocity especially when the topic is important to participants. Researcher acknowledgment of participant experience and expertise brings benefits as follows (McCoyd & Shadaimah, 2007):

- the validation of being understood and of having one's story heard in full without judgment;

- the chance to have one's story joined with others in such a way as to create a "voice" on a topic of shared experience; and

- the knowledge that findings will be published and communicated to providers, policymakers, and the public. (p. x)

For some participants, the opportunity to have a voice possibly affecting policy is a powerful incentive. For example, in my 5-year study of principals' perspectives on a new teacher-evaluation system, the implementation was challenging because data-reporting systems changed; formal observation time increased, limiting time for becoming familiar with students; and the school staff's established educational culture was disrupted. Principals were eager to have their stories told and anticipated my published papers would reach policy makers who might change the policy's negative aspects.

Appreciation of Participants' Time

Qualitative researchers frequently underestimate the amount of time needed to conduct research because of such issues as scheduling interviews and failing to anticipate delays. For example, Joe, a doctoral student, was surprised that when he e-mailed participants in schools they did not respond for several days. If he had checked the school calendar, he would have realized that the school's staff members were focused on annual statewide testing. Staff likely did not read their e-mail for days. Glesne (2016) cautions that because researchers are external they are generally not a priority for participants. Researcher flexibility when contacting participants and scheduling interviews demonstrates understanding. It is not unusual for an interview to be rescheduled because of an emergency or an unexpected event that is a higher priority especially for organizational leaders. Noting priority events and considering their significance might provide a better understanding of the context and people.

Consideration of participant time is also a factor in trust development essential to the researcher–participant relationship. By design, longitudinal studies allow time for trust to develop. While time alone does not guarantee that trust will develop, it does allow participants to see that the researcher keeps promises made at the study's beginning (Glesne, 2016). Demonstrate over time that participants' contributions are valuable in a study.

Understand the Context and Topic

Rapport is enhanced when interviewees know the researcher understands the context. To put participants at ease, the researcher consciously should reflect on their behavior and how they fit into the research context (Glesne, 2016). This behavior includes nonverbal cues, appearance, and attire with the goal of fitting in. Rapport is also developed when participants know that the researcher cares about a topic important to them and desires to assist others in understanding the issues.

Sue, a principal, conducted a yearlong case study of principal leadership. At her dissertation defense, she reported that the principals wanted to discuss leadership extensively with her. Thus, Sue's data was rich with insights and stories because she could relate to the situation. On the other hand, John, a primary teacher in a small school, wanted to study an urban principal who closed a school due to declining enrollment and the school district's boundary reorganization. Because John did not have a background for understanding the principal's role and the complexity of the decisions involved, his study lacked insight and his findings were superficial. While maintaining communication and contact is a way to keep participants involved, ongoing communication during a study can be time consuming. Consistency of the same researcher making contact also sustains a relationship. A regular connection between data collections can minimize the troubling and all-too-common problem of participant attrition (Thomson & Holland, 2003). For example, Thompson and Holland (2003) describe maintaining telephone contact with participants between interviews.

Perceptions of Risks and Benefits to Participants

Evaluating the cost–benefit of proposed research involving human participants is a criterion of ethical decision-making, typically addressed during the institutional review board process. Therefore, before initiating this process, the researcher should consider the potential benefits versus the costs for participants. While much of what is stated here can apply to any qualitative study, the longitudinal method—because of the development of relationships over time—"demands (even produces) a high level of reflexivity on the part of both the researchers and the researched" (Thompson & Holland, 2003, p. 242).

A team of researchers developed a questionnaire to use as an informed data-driven process of determining cost–benefit, rather than as a subjective assessment of whether the proposed research has safeguards protecting human subjects (Newman, Willard, Sinclair, & Kaloupek, 2001). The following three survey items address the benefits from the participant's perspective:

1. Participation—feeling that I made a contribution to an important cause

2. Personal benefits—gaining insight about my experiences through participation

3. In general—believing that the study's results will be useful to others

The second group of survey items identifies a study's risks or costs in time, emotions, or convenience:

4. Negativity—I thought about things I did not want to.

5. Time—The procedures took too long.

6. Questions—Questions were too personal.

7. Participation—Interviews were boring or inconveniently scheduled.

8. Emotions—Unexpected emotional issues, often intense, were raised.

Two additional survey questions are related to trustworthiness:

9. Confidence in the researcher—I believed that my responses would be kept private.

10. Consideration—I felt treated with respect and dignity.

Although potential risks might be perceived by participants as positive, feelings of being part of a cause larger than oneself are a benefit many experience.

ETHICAL CONSIDERATIONS AND DILEMMAS

Researchers must be aware of ethical issues throughout all phases of a research study. Moreover, the possibility of unwelcome intrusion into participants' personal and private lives is greater for qualitative than for quantitative research (Hammersley & Traianou, 2012). Qualitative researchers gain access to people's thoughts and observe what they do. The longitudinal researcher becomes even more immersed in the research and involved with the participants over a longer period, and that involvement can uncover issues not as readily apparent in a short-term study. The longer interaction time with participants also increases familiarity, which generates trust. At the same time, the increased closeness might lead to participants' disclosures about personal matters or sensitive topics. For example, in one of his studies, Saldaña (2003) learned of a young man's drug use, abuse, and attempted suicide. The longer interaction time with participants might also affect the researcher's attitudes, values, and belief systems. For example, observations during fieldwork might conflict with the researcher's beliefs as Saldaña noted by describing what he perceived to be humiliating teacher comments that damaged students' learning experiences. It is clear when an observation of abuse requires a mandatory legal report. Less clear is what the researcher should do when troubling, but not illegal, practices (e.g., humiliating comments) are observed. Saldaña advises treating incidents individually and making a judgment call as deemed necessary. The researcher's goal should be to maintain a professional distance while becoming more immersed in the field context.

Other worrisome roles researchers might confront include those Glesne (2016) describes as *exploiter, reformer,* and *advocate.* Exploiting, or taking advantage of, participants can be subtle. This dilemma can be considered in terms of power and position; that is, the researcher has the power to use the data to reach personal and professional goals while the participant receives little or nothing in return. To resolve this dilemma, Glesne suggests asking how the researcher can give back to the community, referring to those connected by a common interest (e.g., school principals, nurses, or the scientific community).

Advocating for a cause might be tempting when becoming immersed in knowledge of a problem or situation. For example, when studying teacher dismissals, Tom became aware of the sometimes arbitrary judgments involved in performance evaluation. He told me, "That is just wrong," and indicated he might take his concern to a public forum. Like advocacy when the researcher encounters a potentially dangerous situation, reform involves the researcher's intervention to report, expose, or correct activities observed that might be illegal, inhumane, or unethical.

While acting on these situations might seem necessary, one must first decide if such action would best serve others. When faced with an ethical dilemma, a researcher might be best served by seeking advice to make effective decisions. Glesne (2016) suggests forming a support group or panel of experts who could help handle ethical questions that arise. When discussing ethical dilemmas, however, researchers must maintain confidentiality. Ultimately, deciding what to do is a judgment call the researcher should carefully consider.

Exiting the Study

When designing my first longitudinal study, I did not understand that a 5-year research relationship might generate participants' need for closure. However, after examining my notes and reflections, I found that participants expressed enjoyment of the interviews and asked questions about when I planned to visit next. Knowing that many participants have enjoyed and benefitted from the research process, the long-term relationship with participants in an ongoing study requires a strategy for closure or exit.

Research in the field typically ends for participants after data collection is completed. However, when participants have revealed personal information, they can feel abandoned or isolated at the end of the study and can have a strong need to continue (Morrison, Gregory, & Thibodeau, 2012). In their study of overweight adolescent boys, Morrison, Gregory, and Thibodeau (2012) found that communicating at the beginning of the study how and when the study would end was important. Furthermore, they viewed a unilateral exit as unethical as it stemmed from a researcher-centric point of view without participant consideration. These researchers discussed the participants' strong negative emotions when the end of the study and the exit from it approached. During the study, the boys enjoyed and benefitted from the researchers' attention and the opportunity to participate in activities and voice their opinions. However, based on their comments at the study's conclusion, they were angry, sad, and felt let down; and at least one boy felt used or objectified. These feelings conflicted with the trust and rapport developed during the longitudinal research. Consequently, Morrison et al. caution that participants could be harmed or at risk when the need for emotional attention is not recognized. To address these concerns, the researcher should design the exit at the beginning of the study. Additionally, the researcher can negotiate the exit with participants by discussing a smooth, rather than an abrupt, transition. For example, my doctoral student Jenny held weekly meetings in a study of overweight middle school girls. The girls were upset and reluctant to end the supportive discussion sessions. Thus, Jenny agreed to transition to monthly check-in meetings for a specified period and to provide support materials. She also investigated if continuing the meetings with school personnel might be a possibility and spoke with the school counselor.

Considering participants' emotional involvement and need for closure, Morrison et al. (2012) advise institutional review boards to add an exit component to studies involving vulnerable populations. Even if not required by IRBs, an exit strategy should be among the longitudinal researcher's considerations.

Exit interviews can provide participants' perceptions and insights into personal change occurring during the study. Furthermore, the exit interview might also provide the opportunity to add missing data (Saldaña, 2003). In addition, the researcher can obtain useful feedback about the research process and confirm or refute emerging longitudinal themes. Exit interviews can also be beneficial for organizations. For example, over 6 months in three nursing homes, Utley-Smith and colleagues (2006) collected qualitative and quantitative data, including structured interviews with residents, participant observation of staff as they worked, in-depth interviews with staff, and document reviews. In a variation of an exit interview that included consultation, the researchers created and used a presentation. They used the exit presentation for rapidly disseminating research findings to inform organizations. These researchers learned to be more mindful of each organization's dynamics in relation to the data.

Examples of questions from an exit interview with individuals include the following:

- How do you view teacher evaluation differently now than in 2011, prior to the reform implementation?
- How have your beliefs about teacher evaluation changed?
- How did you benefit from research participation during the 5 years?
- What problems did you encounter in participating in the research?

Ongoing contact with research participants generates familiarity affecting the researcher. Over time, this relationship demands and produces a high level of reflexivity (Thompson & Holland, 2003).

Chapter Summary

Researchers will naturally be involved with and focus on their study. However, participants' feelings and needs must be part of a balanced view of the research relationship. This chapter explored many ways to show participants respect and consideration including sharing research results, listening carefully, giving small gifts, respecting their time, and exiting the research mindful of participants' feelings developed during the longitudinal study.

Reflection Questions and Application Activities

- This chapter focuses on the two-way research relationship. In what other ways might you show appreciation and respect for participants' involvement?
- What is the most important concept you learned in this chapter, and why?
- Research and report on your institution's IRB protocol related to longitudinal qualitative studies.

5

MANAGEMENT OF LONGITUDINAL DATA THROUGHOUT A STUDY

In this chapter, the reader will explore

- data-management strategies throughout a study,
- advantages and limitations of data-management software programs, and
- challenges with large data sets.

M anaging accumulated data is necessary in all phases of qualitative longitudinal research. This chapter discusses management considerations in the various stages of a longitudinal qualitative study.

KEEPING CODING TIMELY AND ONGOING

Qualitative longitudinal research poses challenges; but as Barley (1990) notes, "The most daunting occurs after leaving the field, ordering and analyzing what many would consider to be an overwhelming corpus of descriptive data" (p. 234). A researcher must find a way to organize and store data large volumes of data. Although I am reputed to be very organized, challenges arise and difficulties emerge even with careful planning.

The first step in managing an overwhelming corpus of data is to maintain the ongoing organizing, filing, and coding. When conducting my first longitudinal study, I came up short in the timeliness-of-coding category and learned a lesson. The need for organization is obvious to me now; but as a neophyte, I delayed coding transcripts due to other job responsibilities. Coding is best done as soon as possible after collection to manage the volume of data accumulated and in qualitative longitudinal data management, timeliness is essential. Every entry or file should be completed as soon as possible after data collection to prevent an accumulation so large that it is intimidating. Moreover, editing field notes, transcribing data, and ensuring that details are complete will save time later.

I applied for and received a small grant for transcription so that transcripts would be quickly available. I also invested in a recording device with a memory stick that allowed timely data downloading as well as easy and efficient access to audio transcripts. In addition to the organizational benefit, the voice transcripts are readily available for checking accuracy of participants' wording or voice intonation should clarification be required. In my interview with researchers Bruce Barnett and Nathern Okwila, they described their data-management strategies. The following is an excerpt from that interview:

MLD: You said it was a challenge to manage the large amount of data. The longitudinal researcher needs to have an effective way of handling the data. How did you put all the data together?

BB/NO: We organized it to make sense (like organizing state test scores from 2014); it was a lot of work to collect the data from the Texas system. Although it was publicly available, it was not in the format needed. Since this was retrospective—a backward look—we had to find out what data we had for what years. Then the state test had changed. We had to keep things chronological. It wasn't easy. Some teachers had been there for 25 years.

MLD: What helped in the data organization?

BB/NO: We examined interview data and ID'd it right away when it was done. We didn't wait to review. We had many other projects and didn't want to mix it up. Working on it right away helped to not get it lost in other electronic documents. Then we hired a transcriber paid by the university budget—we can use any remaining travel budget for research support. And we had a graduate assistant who helped organize the data.

In another interview, researchers Amy Stich and Kristin Cippolone agreed with the organizational challenges Barnett and Okwila identified:

We struggled early in the project to determine the best way to organize and manage the oceans of data collected across multiple sites over time. Having a strong centralized system for managing and organizing data is essential. Online storage that is secure and accessible to only one or two team members (so that, if working with a team, not all hands are involved in moving data) is important to a well-organized, large-scale project. It is just as important to have clear procedures for submitting audio recordings and anonymized field notes to the person responsible for managing audio files, submitting files for transcription, editing and anonymizing final transcripts, uploading final transcripts to the appropriate digital files, and uploading files to qualitative analysis software.

If you love binders and tabs, take markers in a variety of colors to meetings—and use them, you understand organizational skills. If you equally enjoy spreadsheets and tech tools, you have a head start. However, more is required. Begin with a plan for organizing the data, saving it efficiently, and coding the transcripts.

Managing Longitudinal Interview Data

Interviews are the most frequently used qualitative data-collection tool. Greater effort is needed with interviews in a longitudinal study because data are gathered multiple times over the study's duration (White & Arzi, 2005). Hundreds of hours of transcripts, artifacts, and field notes must be accurately labeled and stored for quick and easy retrieval. Sometimes retrieval occurs after a year or more when memory needs refreshing for clarity and development of themes. Consequently, a large database cannot be discarded even after analysis because questions can emerge requiring a review of the material (White & Arzi, 2005).

I wondered if the longitudinal *qualitative* researcher could learn management lessons from *quantitative* longitudinal researchers. Saldaña (2003), a respected qualitative longitudinal researcher, examined quantitative methods and terms when attempting to find qualitative equivalents but realized that "the exercise was both futile and moot since time and change—including types of change—are contextual to a study" (p. 81). Consequently, the researcher's organizational system must be flexible to accommodate new insights.

Labeling Data

Documentation, critical in managing the vast amounts of longitudinal data, needs to be consistently labeled with time and date. This labeling is not only for the original researcher to retrieve data but also for future researchers to follow the evidence trail and use the data. Saldaña (2003) advises that a longitudinal researcher should be aware of the possible role of historian and document societal, cultural, or political changes at the time of data collection. His point, I believe, is that the researcher is unable to anticipate what may be important to future interpretation and publication. Thus, it is also helpful to label by pseudonym or code assigned to the interviewee. Furthermore, the date of the interview must be noted as well as changes in interviewees' perceptions, which might be connected to events such as introduction of a new policy or program. It is also useful to indicate if more than one interviewer collected data in case an interviewer's interpretation needs to be rechecked during analysis.

EFFECTIVE ORGANIZATION

Manual Coding and Analysis

Binders of printed transcripts take up 2 feet on a shelf in my office. This storage system is useful because I can quickly and easily go to the shelf and find a binder by year and interview. I have also used the method I originally learned: cutting sentences of the transcript to stack and sort under emerging themes. Sometimes the tried and true is necessary. One morning in a discussion, a colleague and I attempted to interpret a study's qualitative comments when differences in interpretation of participants' meanings emerged. Getting close to argumentative, we needed a visual representation to understand the codes and potential themes. I printed the comments, put a shorthand code by each comment identifying participant and date, and then cut the comments into 8 ½ x 3-inch sections. We cleared a space on my office table moving books and papers to the side and stacked comments by code and theme. It was immediately apparent that one category had too many subcodes to be useful. Thus, we further divided, and the light bulb of discovery illuminated the categories that became the foundation of findings in our article. Sometimes color-coding, crayons, and cut-and-paste result in insights that were previously elusive.

When a researcher is stuck on an approach to interpreting voluminous data, a hybrid method using Microsoft Word's comment function can be helpful. I have tried many strategies searching for a management system best suited to my organizational thought process. Early in my longitudinal journey, I took a university-sponsored Atlas TI workshop and then began learning how to use this program to check my manual work. However, in the process, my university purchased NVivo and no longer supported Atlas TI. Rather than diving into learning a new program, I returned to relying on my binders. Yet, after several years of accumulating data, I learned that this single approach was limited. Thus, I supplemented the system of binders with a new software program, realizing again that such a tool has both advantages and limitations.

Using a Qualitative Software Tool: Advantages and Limitations

Methods of reading and coding data range from low to high tech. I have used all of them. Physically manipulating the data, I make copies of the data and cut and divide into data chunks that can be sorted on the wall; on chart paper; or most frequently, on the dining room table. This approach allows me to quickly see which codes have an abundance of comments and which are skimpy. Then I can rearrange the data to assess if something is missing, needs to be subdivided, or perhaps is merely an outlier and not a theme. I had resisted computer-assisted coding and analysis because my previous experience with computer software had led to a superficial result involving a word count and a word search, tasks I could have performed using Microsoft Word. In retrospect, I expected too much from the software too early in the coding and analysis process. A computer-assisted software CAQDAS program becomes indispensable as another tool in longitudinal qualitative studies for organizing massive amounts of narrative data. Computer-assistance programs are best used in the second cycle of coding or grouping previous segments of data into categories and identifying emergent themes.

I found that all computer-assisted qualitative data analysis software has both advantages and limitations, particularly in the early coding stage. I seemed to be mired in learning the technology and being indecisive regarding its use. Then a bright graduate student, Jacob Kamer, was hired by the university and assigned to my department. He was an eager learner and welcomed an opportunity to learn NVivo and assist in a real, not textbook, research application. Jacob was enrolled in a qualitative methodology course and willing to apply his learning. Moreover, he was technologically proficient and embraced the use of a new tool. His positive perspective was

LEARNING NVIVO
LESSONS BY A BEGINNER, FOR A BEGINNER
Jacob Kamer

When I first became involved with Dr. Derrington's research, I had just started the second semester of my PhD program and had just recently received a graduate assistantship. To the field of educational research, I was an eager greenhorn. Naturally, when the opportunity arose to work with Dr. Derrington on a longitudinal qualitative study, I accepted it wholeheartedly. As a part of my new undertaking as a novice researcher, I had a clear task: learn how to use NVivo (a software used for analyzing qualitative data) and identify how it could be used in our longitudinal qualitative research. In this excerpt, I offer advice and share experiences for my fellow novices. By writing this, I hope that my notes prove useful and insightful to those (the researchers and students alike) looking to expand their qualitative data analysis to a digital platform such as NVivo.

Understand What You Want to Accomplish

NVivo is a powerful tool for organizing, analyzing, and manipulating qualitative data. As such, it has the capability to perform a myriad of basic, intermediate, and advanced functions. When I first downloaded NVivo, I explored and practiced with a variety of its functions, many of which were critical to our project and many more of which were fascinating but overall unnecessary. Depending on the needs of your research project, you (the researcher) may only need the most basic functions NVivo offers, such as text search, word frequencies, brainstorming (mind maps), and coding (nodes). More advanced operations—such as cross-tabulations (matrix coding) and relationships— may be imperative or superfluous depending on the research project. Prior to downloading NVivo (or another analytical software), you should have a general idea of what you need it for and what specific functions you would like it to perform.

Know What Resources Are Free and Convenient

Along with beginning with the end in mind, you should become aware of what resources are available (particularly those that are free and convenient) that will help you to navigate NVivo and to make your analysis more efficient. From creating concept maps to building nodes and running queries, I had no idea where to turn first. Fortunately, I did not spin my metaphorical wheels too long; I had excellent (and free) resources at my disposal to help me get started. After a couple of meetings with the

(Continued)

(Continued)

University of Tennessee's resident expert on NVivo, I was able to start making progress. In addition to expert consultation, I viewed (and reviewed) numerous NVivo tutorials on YouTube. For any researchers or students lacking access to an NVivo expert on campus, the YouTube tutorials are of particular import. Clicking the link for *Tutorials* on the NVivo home screen will directly forward you to these YouTube videos, which cover material on both basic and advanced NVivo functions. Using on-campus resources and calling upon YouTube videos, however, are only just the beginning. QSR International, NVivo's developer, offers a number of free webinars for NVivo subscribers. If your organization or university has an NVivo subscription, you may wish to check into any complimentary interactive webinars or tutorials offered directly through QSR International. In short, if you intend to use NVivo (or a comparable platform) for qualitative data analysis, dedicate time to investigating and making use of complimentary resources.

Before starting out on the search for NVivo resources, however, take note of what operating system you (alone or with your research team) plan to use. The Windows and Mac versions of NVivo are generally incompatible with one another; separate tutorials and resources exist for both options. When collaborating with multiple researchers or authors who might be using different operating systems, you may find this particular aspect of NVivo to prove challenging.

Test the Waters Before Diving Into Them

Once you have an idea of what you need NVivo to do and what resources are available to you for support, you may wish to try your hand at using NVivo before jumping into any detailed analysis of your data. Rather than doing this with interview transcripts or other qualitative sources (audio recordings, videos, pictures, etc.) pertaining to your research project, you may wish to practice with a sample project. Once you open NVivo, an option should appear on the home screen labeled *Sample Project*. When I was first learning the ins and outs of NVivo, this function proved invaluable to me. The sample project will open with example sources (photos, interview transcripts, audio recordings, video, etc.), memos, and articles preloaded, along with helpful hints and a list of steps to help you get started with analyzing qualitative data in NVivo. Understandably, not every researcher will be able to dedicate ample amounts of time to practice using a sample project. Some practice using an example project, however, should make data analysis on the actual research project more efficient and less taxing.

much needed. The combination of my experience and understanding of methodology with his computer expertise led to a productive collaboration. However, even with a predisposition to embrace software, initial learning and eventual mastery take time and patience as Jacob relates in the accompanying reflections on learning NVivo.

A Useful Learning and Teaching Resource

In my longitudinal journey, I discovered that my university library subscribed to the SAGE research platform, an excellent resource for students and teachers. One resource in the collection contains cases illustrating how methods are applied in research projects. The case studies highlight project design and methods' application through stories of real-life research. These cases illustrate the practicalities and challenges of conducting research using various methodologies. They also demonstrate the obstacles and choices researchers face when their project moves from paper to the often-messy world of data collection. The SAGE cases are selected from a broad variety of sources across the spectrum of academic disciplines, business, sociology, anthropology, and political science. They can be used by students to illuminate research approaches and by professors to teach various research methodologies. The cases can be selected by discipline, academic level, and methodology.

Source: http://methods.sagepub.com.proxy.lib.utk.edu:90/Search/SavedSearch/1253

See Appendix A for a sample, *Picturing Policy Implementation: An Ethnography of a Local Network,* by Pam Carter.

Additional resources are available to practice applying skills to a data set. I explored SAGE Research Methods Datasets, a collection of teaching datasets and instructional guides that give students a chance to learn data analysis through practice. Students can see how analytic decisions are made, helping them to become confident researchers.

Possible activities using this resource include the following:

- practicing qualitative and quantitative analytical methods with sample data and instructional guides;

- finding datasets that demonstrate dozens of methods and represent work in business, education, health, political science, psychology, and sociology; and

- finding downloadable data to use in course assignments and exam questions.

I appreciate new resources to assist me in the role of researcher, teacher, and learner.

Interview on Managing, Coding, and Analyzing Data

The following excerpt from an interview with Stich and Cippolone provides another glimpse into data management as well as data coding and analysis, topics explored in the next chapter.

MLD: Please tell me more how you analyzed the data. You created themes perhaps, but how did you put all of them and the data you had together? Across the data for findings?

AS/KC: Members of our team engaged in data analysis in phases over time and across sites. Because one academic year constituted one distinct segment of time in our analysis, we coded data during and after each particular year we were engaged in the study. Analysis across schools was treated similarly to a multicase study approach, as we coded participant and observation data within each particular site separately, developing categories and themes before making cross-case comparisons. Two of our four schools in each city were STEM-focused schools, and two were comprehensive high schools; so particular comparisons were made between institutions that were similar in structure and aims and those that were distinctly different. We then repeated the same process in years 2 and 3, making cross-case comparisons over time. While data were coded each year, codes remained consistent, which allowed us to analyze across years. As part of the larger comparative project, teams shared findings and worked together to produce findings across cities over time.

Chapter Summary

All research, like learning itself, is a process, a journey of discovery. However, the longitudinal researcher's journey is longer. As a result, greater attention must be given to effective organization and data details. The researcher has flexibility to create a personally effective organizational schema. The common denominators among schemas are ensuring data accuracy, timeliness, retention, and retrievability.

Reflection Questions and Application Activities

- Compare manual coding of qualitative data with computer-assisted coding. What are the strengths and limitations of each approach?

- What is the most powerful idea you took away from this chapter?

- How can you apply the information to a study you are considering?

6

LONGITUDINAL DATA ANALYSIS

In this chapter, the reader will

- explore approaches to data analysis,

- review types of visual representations, and

- examine the importance of considering significant events that researchers experience when conducting qualitative longitudinal studies.

Excellent texts are available on qualitative data analysis. However, this chapter adds the longitudinal perspective by considering analysis issues when a study extends beyond a year, or two data collections, and includes multiple participants.

APPROACHES TO DATA ANALYSIS

Analysis involves judgments about how to reduce and organize the large dataset collected in a longitudinal study and to transform the data into meaningful interpretations (Glesne, 2016; Rossman & Rallis, 2012). In approaching my own longitudinal study, I searched for but found little guidance on conducting an analysis involving multiple participants and spanning years. While most authors discussed a single study, I needed a way to scale up a study analyzing 14 participants over 5 years of interviews. In the first 2 years of my analysis, dividing the body of research into smaller units worked well. I could easily examine and compare responses to individual questions across 2 years. In subsequent years, however, examining smaller units seemed repetitive with no new emerging insights.

I understood that an enormous amount of data could lead to deeper insights by viewing change through key issues and themes emerging over time. However, when findings became repetitive, I experienced "analysis paralysis"; thus, a fresh approach was required. Until then, I had used printed transcripts to sort and analyze the database manually as I had done with smaller scale studies. Yet, I suspected this method alone was insufficient for deeply understanding change in teacher evaluation. My concern was reinforced when the first article based on the entire 5-year study was returned with the following peer review:

> The analysis and conclusion come across essentially as syntheses of the data and do not in any way suggest that you have been engaged in these settings over 5 years. That they do not draw back on this substantial body of research is a shame. Revising the analysis and conclusion sections of the paper to draw on this body of research could demonstrate the significance of the study for policymaking as well as for future research.

After healing my wounded author ego, I reread the comments and knew that the reviewer was correct. Digging deeper into the data was necessary, but how to do so was unclear. After searching for *the* answer in textbooks and journals and seeking colleagues' advice, I discovered that data can be analyzed through several approaches, which can be borrowed from a range of traditions and disciplines. Among the various approaches is the use of themes, questions, and theoretical triangulation, as well as multiple views and multiple analysts.

Theming With a Longitudinal Perspective

Themes are the vehicle through which a researcher filters data on the journey of understanding change. A solid grounding in single-study theme development is a good foundation for delving into longitudinal qualitative analysis. Understanding how to create and analyze themes is the starting point for launching into more complex analysis of a large qualitative dataset. The following excerpts from published studies provide examples of a thematic approach to longitudinal analysis.

Example 1

In a study of the effectiveness of a job-retention and rehabilitation pilot program, Lewis (2007) discusses her analysis process. First, reading and rereading were necessary to become familiar with the data. Next, key themes were identified and divided into a series of subtopics. Then a series of matrices was created, each displaying one theme. Columns in the matrix represented subtopics and rows represented interviews. Each chart had one row for each of the six interviews. The first chart also incorporated a summary of each participant's interview at each of the six interview stages. The fifth chart was a "whole case summary" completed after the sixth interview.

Example 2

In a study of hospital nurses' emotional reactions to the experience of organizational change, Giaever and Smollan (2015) read interview transcripts several times during the multiple data-collection points. Then to deepen their understanding and support their analysis of the interview data, they isolated passages indicating emotional reactions to changes. Next, they reread those passages and formed a set of codes or categories (initial coding generation) indicating the participants' emotions (e.g., joy, anger, insecurity) at each data collection point. After becoming familiar with the data, they coded and then reviewed, labeled, and developed themes. Following theme development, they searched for patterns and intensity of the identified emotions. Then they explored the development of emotions, looking for similarities and differences among the themes represented in the first, second, and third interviews. These researchers were interested in examining how and in what ways emotions changed, or did not change, over time. They presented findings in two tables, the first illustrating the themes and the second showing themes common to all three data-collection points.

Example 3

A study of the perspectives of people with progressively severe chronic obstructive pulmonary disease (COPD) involved analysis of data when several groups of participants are involved (Pinnock et al., 2007). Four interviews with three groups of participants were conducted over 18 months. The groups included 21 patients, 13 informal caregivers (e.g., friends), and 19 professional caregivers (e.g., nurses). The interview data from each group were analyzed and coded separately. After developing themes, the researchers compared and contrasted themes within and across each dataset to highlight emergent themes and divergent perspectives. Several visual representations were used to illustrate the findings including a table with column headings for the interview date, a quotation illustrating the theme, context, and fieldnotes. An additional table illustrated differences and similarities among patients' perspectives and those of the formal and informal caregivers. The third visual reflected research questions with themes and the participants' narratives.

Questions Framing Change

Longitudinal qualitative analysis benefits from questions regarding change in an individual or an organization (Vallance, 2005). Questions can assist the researcher to develop in-depth analysis and richer interpretations. Furthermore, questions provide clues to understanding change as the researcher moves from coding data to creating meaning. Although a researcher will eventually develop useful unique questions, beginning with example questions from experienced qualitative longitudinal researchers can be helpful. Some analytical questions the researcher can consider include the following:

- What increases or emerges through time?

- What is cumulative through time?

- What kind of surges, epiphanies, or turning points occur through time?

- What decreases or ceases through time?

- What remains constant or consistent through time?

- What is idiosyncratic through time?

- What is missing through time?

These questions are suggestions, not prescriptive or formulaic steps (Saldaña, 2003, 2016).

Moreover, these questions apply to studies examining organizational change and perspectives of change. The following questions can be useful when studying change in individuals:

- What contextual and interviewing conditions appear to influence and affect participant change(s) through time?

- What are the dynamics of participant change(s) through time? (Saldaña, 2003)

However, answers to the questions regarding individual change cannot be viewed in isolation as the interrelationship of events and dynamics should be examined through time (Saldaña, 2003). Events such as a significant social, political, or personal milestone can affect participants' beliefs or behaviors and, consequently, have implications for interpretation. A turning point or critical incident experienced by a participant and documented in the data could be significant if it produces sudden changes in the participant's actions. As Saldaña (2003) notes, "significance is in the eye of the participant" (p. 110), meaning that the researcher might interpret an event as unimportant although it is significant to the participant. When using questions to analyze data, I have learned to watch for flashes of insight and to scrutinize interview data for words indicating a significant event. Important events might be big life moments, such as a child's birth or a new work-related significant occurrence, such as a new supervisor with a different philosophy from the previous boss. Sometimes, however, an important event might be interpreted as mundane and go unrecognized. For example, I observed a new teacher struggling with classroom management and discipline. Then one day I realized that her chaotic approach had changed into consistent, positive behavioral interventions. In an interview, she mentioned reading a book on positive reinforcement. At first, I viewed this comment as unimportant; but upon analysis, I realized it was a critical event for that teacher. Later in another interview, the teacher confirmed that the book significantly altered her philosophy of and approach to classroom management. Applying a variety of change-centered questions prompts the researcher to consider analysis in numerous ways.

Building on useful analysis questions, Vallance (2005) suggests examining causality and generalization. For example, noting comments on participants' perceptions, a researcher might develop a question related to the observed changes' causes. Moreover, comparing themes of change permits the researcher to develop hypotheses related to why these changes are occurring. Before ending a study, a researcher can test the hypotheses in discussions with participants. Vallance also suggests that a researcher can examine the extent to which changes are general or universal rather than particular or individualistic. While this approach may appear contrary to the qualitative researcher's grounding in context, Vallance suggests that a notion of universal change might result from a detailed examination of the relationship among patterns, the researcher's perspectives, and fieldnotes. The following are additional analytical questions the researcher can consider:

- What has changed?
- How has it changed?

- Why has it changed?
- For whom has it changed?
- How have they changed? (Vallance, 2005)

Theoretical Triangulation

Theoretical triangulation allows a researcher to examine data from multiple frameworks, thus expanding interpretations. The purpose is to gain new knowledge and insight, in contrast to *data triangulation* that uses different data sources to confirm or disconfirm findings. Rossman and Rallis (2017) suggest examining the link between a theme and a theory using theoretical memo writing during theme analysis. In addition, examining multiple theoretical frames controls researcher overreach and assists in avoiding bias. Theoretical frames can be adopted from others or developed from the researcher's deep knowledge of the topic. Explaining how themes tie into theories and how the author views the importance of conclusions is part of the analysis using a theoretical triangulation approach (Miles & Huberman, 1994).

Multiple Views

Viewing data in multiple ways assists the researcher to deepen understanding and to develop a holistic perspective. A researcher can examine data sequentially, cyclically, or by components. For example, I examined each year of principals' interview data separately to identify similarities and differences. These data could be further analyzed in discrete sections—for example, by grade level or gender. Viewing the data holistically requires considering inextricably embedded contexts as a dynamic of the longitudinal change process (Saldaña, 2002). For example, the classroom context for a teacher might include the students, the curriculum, a supervisor, and resources. These context elements might be viewed as intervening circumstances, depending on researcher interpretation: "There is a specific history and course of events to every particular participant, every particular setting, every particular researcher, and every particular study" (Saldaña, 2003, p. 82). As an example, in my Washington women's superintendent study, the differences in family lifestyles in 1993, 2009, and 2017 might have been influenced by women's larger societal issues. Although I did not document social and political events during the earliest study, a careful reading of historical and political events at the time would provide insightful background information.

Multiple Analysts Collaboration

The quantity of qualitative longitudinal data frequently requires two or more researchers' collaboration throughout the study. Involving multiple researchers in the analysis stage can be both beneficial and challenging. One benefit is that multiple researchers' perspectives add to the interpretation of findings. Additionally, multiple viewpoints can decrease subjectivity and minimize bias. Moreover, different perspectives result in a deeper understanding and discussion of the topic. For example, John, my frequent collaborator, is a school assistant superintendent. His view of teacher evaluation is rooted in daily observations of principals' supervision and evaluation practices. The combination of his experience and my knowledge of research design has grounded our teacher evaluation studies and is relevant to both a practitioner and an academic audience. On the other hand, researchers might work with data coders or analysts unfamiliar with the research topic. I used this strategy after receiving a grant to code and theme a large amount of qualitative longitudinal data. The new researchers had no background in my topic and little understanding of the terms and references in the data. If I had provided a background briefing early in the study, they would have had the necessary information for understanding the context. On the other hand, their fresh, context-free perspectives resulted in interesting observations as well as new connections and questions.

Involving many analysts also presents challenges. Sometimes perspectives are difficult to resolve, leading to wasted time, hurt feelings, or abandonment of the project. As with all interactions, respectful listening and humility in presenting points of view are necessary for good collaborations. Researchers must be mindful that there is not just one correct interpretation of data. Instead, there are likely different interpretations of the responses to the multiple questions asked (Kvale, 1996).

A method to merge and coordinate the various perspectives is required. The lead researcher can be tasked with the primary responsibility of organizing collaborators, scheduling due dates, and making final decisions. Stich and Cippolone (2017) illustrate collaborative steps in their study. After approximately 200 subcodes were developed, team members read a quarter of all the interviews. The authors report, "Coding schema emerged from joint discussions of the individual codes. Upon agreement, codes were then applied to the remaining interview data" (p. 11).

An interview with Stich further illustrates the nature of collaboration.

We struggled early in the project to determine the best way to organize and manage the "oceans of data" collected across multiple sites over time. Although we ultimately dealt with the challenges, it took strong teamwork and respectful and consistent discussion both within and across teams in Buffalo and Denver to rise to this challenge. It is also important to note that our work represents just one type of longitudinal study and the collaborative team-based dimension of this project presented different kinds of challenges than those faced by individuals taking on longitudinal projects.

VISUAL REPRESENTATIONS

Using a variety of visual representations can uncover deeper meanings and reveal relationships among the data parts (Kvale, 1996). Visualizing data assists both readers and researchers in organizing, classifying, and finding patterns of meaningful connections (Glesne, 2017). Creating visuals also facilitates thinking about relationships among data segments such as years or participants. Pondering the importance of rubrics in teacher evaluation, I wrestled with the underlying reasons that principals, year after year, continued reporting rubric significance. Early one morning with a second cup of coffee in hand, I visualized diagramming a sentence. Experimenting with a diagram spurred new thoughts on relationships within my longitudinal research. As an example, see Figure 1.

This diagram assisted me in framing relationships in my data. However, readers might respond differently. I shared my flash of insight with a colleague, who silently looked at it for some time before telling me that the visual did not work for him. When I placed the same information into

FIGURE 1 ■ Sentence Diagram of Time Commitment

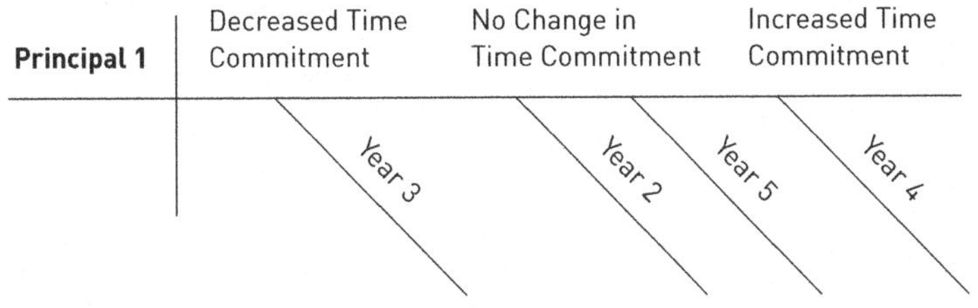

a chart, my colleague thought the information was clearer. I learned that readers respond differently to various types of visuals, so it is best to use a variety, such as concept maps, matrices, word clouds, project maps, correlations, and hierarchy charts.

Concept Maps

As Novak (2005) illustrated, concepts maps can demonstrate the relationship development to understand students' acquisition of science knowledge over time. While the process was time intensive, he reported that making a concept map from interview transcripts provided a visual for following change in students' knowledge progressing through grades levels.

Concept maps can be developed in NVivo, but the researcher must be familiar with the data and knowledgeable of the relationships among components. To explore early ideas about the research or to brainstorm without digging deeply into the data, a researcher may wish to explore a mind map in NVivo, which allows the user to illustrate preliminary thoughts and potential connections. Once the researcher explores the data, he or she may illustrate the narrative (or at least a portion of it). Because of the mass amount of data generated during a qualitative longitudinal study, the researcher may describe sections of the narrative first. Based on data collected through my qualitative longitudinal teacher evaluation study, I generated a concept map (Figure 2) to depict a principal's perception of relationship changes across time.

Matrices

A matrix illustrates study elements through rows and columns that can be combined in various ways. Miles, Huberman, and Saldaña (2014) illustrate the concept of using a time-ordered meta-matrix to analyze qualitative data. Using data from my research, I sought to expand this approach to a longitudinal study. I examined interview transcripts from one participant across the study's 5 years and mapped out the development of themes (See Table 1). The blackened box indicate a theme's absence in the data analysis.

Word Clouds

Word clouds (available through NVivo) can be used to illustrate the most frequently occurring words within a transcript or document. In creating a word cloud, the researcher should specify the number of words to include so that the final product is not unreadable or unwieldy (e.g., selecting the top 100 most frequent words versus the top 1,000). The researcher should also avoid including the wording of interview questions or other nonresponse text

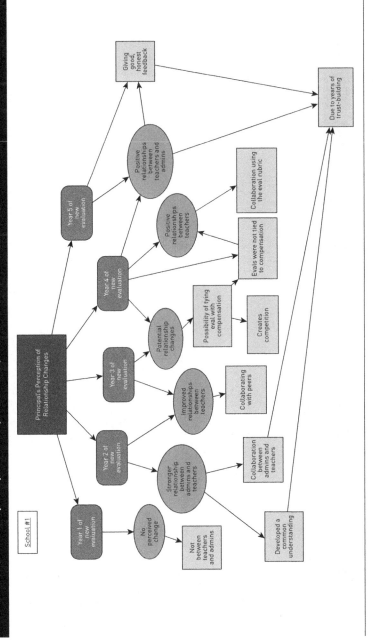

School #1

TABLE 1 ■ Theme Development Matrix

Themes	Year 1	Year 2	Year 3	Year 4	Year 5
Learning to Incorporate Process and Demands	Overcoming a learning curve Becoming more familiar with the process	Improving consistency in evaluations Working the maze	Coordinating evaluation efforts		Coordinating evaluation efforts Becoming more familiar with the process
Managing Time and Change	Concerns with the number of evaluations Many changes over a short amount of time	Challenges managing other job duties Challenges managing personal life	Decreased time commitment	Increased time commitment Needs consistency	No change in time commitment Depends more on a calendar
Focusing on the Bigger Education Picture	Focusing efforts on broader issues	Taking broad ownership of the evaluation		Concerned about getting distracted from more important issues	Responsibility as a leader Understanding highly effective instruction
Relationships	No perceived changes in relationships	Stronger relationships between teachers and admins Improved relationships between teachers	Improved relationships between teachers	Positive relationships between teacher Positive relationships between teachers and admins	Positive relationships between teachers and admins

in the word cloud's analysis. From a longitudinal perspective, word clouds can be useful for a cursory examination of differences in word frequency during individual years and across time. Figures 3 and 4 are examples.

FIGURE 3 ■ Word Cloud of One Transcript in One Year

FIGURE 4 ■ Word Cloud of Multiple Transcripts Across Five Years

Project Maps

Project maps are useful in longitudinal research to illustrate the connections or relationships among multiple sources across time. The sources can include transcripts, or documents, and participants' responses. The following project map (Figure 5) provides an example from my teacher evaluation study. The themes and codes represented by circles and lines correspond to the information from the respondent's transcript.

Correlations

NVivo can provide correlational statistics (e.g., Pearson's *r*) to demonstrate the correlation of transcripts based on either words or nodes (coding). Table 2 illustrates such an example from my study.

Hierarchy Charts

A hierarchy chart (or a sunburst diagram) is helpful in depicting a theme's composition and the proportion of nodes (or codes) in that theme. From a longitudinal perspective, the composition of themes could be compared across participants and across years. Figures 6 and 7 illustrate two different views using hierarchy charts.

These examples are not an exhaustive menu for visual displays but are a selection of some of those available to researchers. Longitudinal qualitative analysis requires using more than one medium, including manual displays of data, color-coding, and NVivo or other computer-assisted programs. While digital tools are helpful, the researcher decides what data to code and use and how to analyze and report results (Glesne, 2016). The most important analysis instrument, however, is the researcher's mind. Qualitative longitudinal analysis requires deep data knowledge acquired through repeated and careful readings of the text. No computer programs can replace this step.

TABLE 2 ■ Correlations by Word Use Among Transcripts Across Years		
Source A	**Source B**	**Pearson Correlation Coefficient**
Year 2	Year 1	0.813
Year 2	Year 3	0.682
Year 2	Year 4	0.674
Year 2	Year 5	0.681

FIGURE 5 ■ Project Map

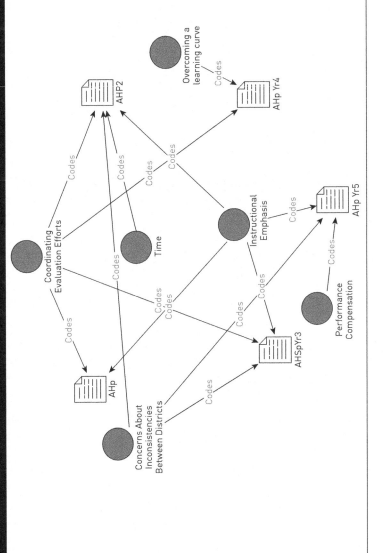

FIGURE 6   ■   Hierarchy Chart Example

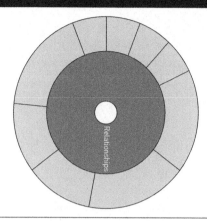

FIGURE 7   ■   Hierarchy Chart With Nodes Expanded

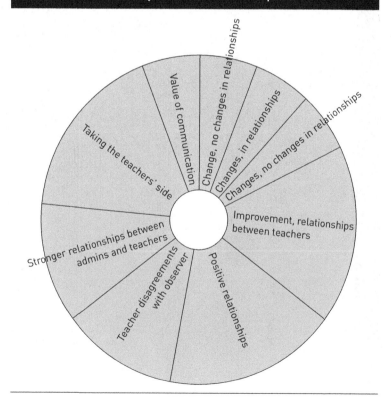

Chapter Summary

Multilayered data and their analysis make longitudinal qualitative research complex and challenging. However, embracing the challenge and finding methods to handle complexity results in a deeper analysis of change as it unfolds. Such methods include creating detailed themes, questions, and visual representations, among others. Analysis is more than description; it is a researcher's explanation to readers of various backgrounds and with different experiences. A researcher has a responsibility to convey a clear and thoughtful analysis of data in multiple ways.

Reflection Questions and Application Activities

- This chapter describes theming as a beneficial way to analyze data. Research and describe another way qualitative longitudinal data can be analyzed. Find examples in your discipline of study detailing analysis of qualitative longitudinal data.

- After conducting annual focus groups for the past 3 years, you are ready to begin data analysis. Considering that the qualitative data you have collected spans multiple years, how would you approach coding and theming the data? How would you present the results?

- Which visual in this chapter made the most sense to you and why? In what other ways might qualitative longitudinal date be visualized?

PREPARING A
LONGITUDINAL STUDY
FOR PUBLICATION

In this chapter, the reader will consider

- creation of a meaningful final manuscript,
- words conveying the longitudinal message, and
- examples from published studies.

At last the volume of data is organized and analyzed. However, now is not the time to rest. Research findings continue to influence the manuscript long after data collection and analysis. The written text is an important communication instrument and knowledge source (Flick, 2014). Ensuring that the text conveys important messages requires an understanding of a manuscript's many elements. Writing links the research process and analysis, thus shaping the researcher's "clumps of carefully organized data" (Glesne 2016, p. 218). The first step is finding the emotional connection in what is otherwise an accumulation of words. *Feeling* and *thinking* might not be typically associated with research, yet they can open new ways of writing about longitudinal qualitative studies.

DIGGING DEEPLY FOR MEANING

I watched a piano teacher instruct a young student playing a difficult piece. Although the student was technically competent, his rendition was uninspiring and lacked emotion. The teacher explained how music must be felt to evoke listeners' emotions. Later when I heard the new interpretation evidenced in tempo, rhythm, and intensity, it seemed that stirring a music listener's feelings is like creating meaningful text for readers. Consider the following evocative headings from a study of school reform (Stich & Cipollone, 2017).

The Dizzying Nature of Change: Turnaround and Turnover

A Culture of Continuous Curricular Change

A Revolving Door

Counselors: Overburdened and Underprepared

These headings convey the frustrating problems with school reform found in the study. The authors note that these insights and findings would not have been attainable without the qualitative longitudinal framework that provided breadth and qualitative depth.

Students in research courses become competent in technical aspects of qualitative research as they master data collecting, coding, and theming. Akin to musical interpretation, interpreting research elements tells a story, thus transforming a report to a meaningful translation of events (Rossman & Rallis, 2012; Saldaña, 2015).

To become a meaning maker and ultimately interpret a theme of change, I suggest that a researcher think in new interdisciplinary ways to experience those aha moments that transform a technically sound study into a ground-breaking publication. In his book *Thinking Qualitatively: Methods of Mind,* Saldaña elaborates on numerous ways of thinking and adds application exercises to elicit researcher awareness of the multiple lenses, filters, and angles applicable in a study. I found the chapter "Thinking Multidisciplinarily" particularly helpful in interpreting longitudinal studies and work that "cross boundaries to find multiple connections between phenomena and explanations" (p. 96). Reading widely in other disciplines assists in making connections leading to transformative interpretations of a study.

However, with a full load of graduate courses and a professorial scholarship agenda, making time for additional reading might seem impossible. One method I learned is to create learning opportunities through informal connections. For example, during a break in a Faculty Senate

OPPORTUNITY TO LEARN QUESTIONS

I read your longitudinal study on organizational change. What readings led you to the use of the chaotic change theory?

I was intrigued by your session on lack of substantive change in schools following a reform. What is your direction for continuing this study?

I am researching principals changing perspectives of teacher evaluation. I respect your knowledge of longitudinal research. Do you recommend a book or an article on analyzing a large amount of data?

meeting, a conversation with a law school professor led to my refining a policy perspective with which I had struggled to frame an elusive finding. I had developed questions related to my research to ask if the opportunity arose at conferences in the exhibit hall or during breaks between sessions. While this approach may be off-putting and appear destined to leave the inquisitor alone by the coffee urn, the opposite is true when phrasing questions in terms of someone else's expertise. Discerning ways others think can assist the longitudinal researcher's quest for insight and understanding of change. Some questions I found useful in learning from others are presented.

Writing Manuscripts Incorporating Longitudinality

Creating a meaningful manuscript begins by building well-written article sections. Each section contributes to the connectivity readers rely on for interpreting a large longitudinal data set. Longitudinal writing focuses on words that contribute to an understanding of change and that communicate the change's effects over time. Since time is essential to the longitudinal study, words and phrases indicating change are used throughout the study. Such words and phrases as the following guide readers: *in the beginning, as the year progressed, midway through year 3, during, throughout, toward, after the first year, substantial progress, by the end.* The following publication excerpts illustrate the use of such wording (Stich & Cipollone, 2017):

> Our extended stay in the field allowed us to observe the breakdown of counseling support. In 3 years, we witnessed three different counseling arrangements. In Year 1, Tabitha and Benjamin split

the school equally by alphabet. In Year 2 of the study, Tabitha was given sole responsibility of the high school while Benjamin assumed responsibility for Grades 5 through 8. In Year 3, this arrangement continued, except that Benjamin took over high school test administration. The following year, Tabitha left, and Benjamin again split the counseling load with a new counselor, who was in her first full-time position. Simultaneously, College Board pulled back its support. Counselors received intermittent support in the second year of our study and none in the third year.

A longitudinal study has multiple data collection points; and findings can be reported following logical points—for example, Phases I, II, and III. Some longitudinal studies examine a program's implementation, and data might be collected at the beginning, then midway, and again at the completion of implementation. The following example illustrates such a timeline.

A study of women recently exposed to partner abuse collected data in three interviews across 1 year. The researchers' purpose was to examine the effects of participating in the research. After the initial interview, data collection occurred at 6 and 12 months (Hebenstreit & DePrince, 2012). The published study did not indicate the researchers' reason for the time intervals. However, the extensive literature review or previous similar studies might have influenced the timing of data collection. In addition, the authors reasoned that a year was sufficient for participants to reflect on the incident. When reporting, one caution is to consider retrospective bias. Over time, recollecting an incident is less reliable; thus, the reporting of that incident might also be less accurate (Bolger & Laurenceau, 2013).

Presenting Findings: Describing Change

Headings and subheadings in a research report's finding section can be arranged sequentially by years as the following example illustrates. In a study of principals' perceptions and behaviors during the first 3 years of implementing a new teacher-evaluation system, my colleague and I used Hall and Hord's (2015) Stages of Concern (SoC) framework (Derrington & Campbell, 2015). Since the stage model involved a sequence of years, findings were organized accordingly. Each year was divided into two subheadings reflecting the two research questions: (1) principals' perceptions of teacher-evaluation implementation using Hall and Hord's (2015) SoC framework; and (2) support that principals received, or hoped to receive, throughout the implementation. The term *intervention* was used to describe support from outside people or agencies.

The following subheadings used in a study of school reform were based on a combination of a sequential description and a framework (Peck & Reitzug, 2017):

Developing Connections in Year 1

Navigating Cultural Difference

Important Community Spaces

Writing the Report: Finding One's Voice and Audience

In high school, I liked music and was a fair vocalist. Aspiring to perform in the local theater, I enrolled in voice lessons. In the first lesson, my teacher assessed my range with my repetitive *do re mi* up and down the scale. Vocal exercises determined I was an alto, not a soprano, as I uncomfortably strained when trying to hit the high notes. Then we experimented with everything from style-happy Rodgers and Hammerstein show tunes to dramatic Italian opera arias. After trial and error, my most comfortable style became what I enjoyed most and was the best at delivering. So it is with a writing style. Once a personal preference and strength is identified, writing becomes more pleasurable than painful.

Voice is more than grammar; it is engaging "the reader through rich description, thoughtful sequencing, appropriate use of quotes, and contextual clarity so that the reader joins the inquirer in the search for meaning" (Patton, 2002, p. 65). In determining voice, the writer must also consider the manuscript's intended audience. An academic journal has a different purpose than a practitioner's publication; thus, the choice of first-person high reflexivity versus formal, impersonal third-person wording depends on the targeted journal. Some journals encourage less formality and writing for a practitioner audience. Others prefer manuscripts with a scientific tone.

The following passage illustrates the effective use of first-person plural:

Here, we reveal what happened under the guise of inclusive STEM-focused schooling, highlighting the mechanisms that underlie the dissolution of envisioned reforms in each city. Although researchers who have investigated the fate of recent educational reform efforts in the United States might predict this outcome, our comparative and longitudinal perspective enables us to unravel how rearrangement and redefinition of opportunity structures—away from intended reforms—can occur. In the section that follows, we first briefly describe our larger study and the two cities in which it took place. We then describe the school site selection process in each city, introduce the schools, and present our data collection and analysis methods. (Weis et al., 2015)

Before submitting an article, an author should also consider the aim and scope of the journal and of previously published manuscripts. Most journals' websites detail author guidelines. For example, SAGE has a two-page publication titled "How to Get Your Journal Article Published" (see boxed excerpt) at https://us.sagepub.com/sites/default/files/how_to_get_published.pdf.

The SAGE guidelines outline expectations for academic journal articles.

SAGE guidelines begin with a question for checking a submission. Have you conformed to the conventions of academic writing?

- Introduction with a clear, compelling statement of purpose

- Conceptual grounding/literature review

- Hypotheses/research questions that are clear, meaningful, answerable, inter-related, flow logically from the introduction

- Methodology, appropriate sample, do the procedures/measures offer enough information for replicability/trust

- Analysis and discussion—they should be systematic, sensible analyses

- Results, discussion of results, key findings

- Conclusion: Don't merely repeat results; directives of research and practice; awareness of limitations; don't go beyond the evidence.

In contrast, *Educational Leadership* publishes for a practitioner audience as the following website excerpt indicates.

WHAT WE LOOK FOR

Most published articles are written in a conversational style, and cover topics that are useful for PreK–12 educators. These are some of the qualities we look for:

(Continued)

(Continued)

- Articles describing research-based solutions to current problems in education

- Opinion pieces that interweave experiences and ideas

- Program descriptions (school, district, or state)

- Practical examples that illustrate key points

- An emphasis on explaining and interpreting research results rather than on methodology

Source: http://www.ascd.org/Publications/Educational-Leadership/Guidelines-for-Writers/Guidelines-for-Educational-Leadership-Writers.aspx

Conveying Change and Longitudinality

Words matter, and a thesaurus or the thesaurus function in Word is essential to move from coding data to writing the final manuscript. Word choice becomes even more significant in conveying, not losing, meaning. Choosing words carefully is important but can be a struggle. For example, one day my colleague and I debated the interpretation of data collected. After reading transcripts on teacher evaluation, my colleague exclaimed, "Ah! Over time teachers have less trust in the instrument." Perplexed, I challenged his interpretation by saying, "Use of the word *trust* or even a synonym doesn't show up over the years; we can't say that, we need evidence from the transcript." Upon reflection, my strict interpretation could lead to a superficial report of the findings, while his inference might be jumping to unwarranted conclusions. Patton (2002) offers a cautionary lesson in neutrality when he emphasizes that researchers must neither approach studies with predetermined results in mind nor attempt to reinforce their own perspectives. Such subjectivity might appear easy to avoid. My experience, however, is that bias is easier to identify in others than in ourselves. First, a researcher chooses a topic because he believes it is important and frequently has experience with it. These are good reasons to select a topic but also potential sources of bias. For example, I had breadth and depth of experience in evaluating teachers as a former school administrator. Moreover, I chose my research topic because it interested me and would continue to interest me over the study's multiple years. My background assisted me in digging deeply into the literature order in to stay current. Yet I worried about bias in data analysis and interpretation, so I relied on several methods to achieve a balanced perspective.

I invited a current school administrator to join me in discussing what I had heard in interviews to ground my interpretation of perception in the field. I remained open-minded and curious about changes in the teacher evaluation system since I was a principal. I attended sessions on the topic at professional conferences and then contacted the presenters to ask questions or to clarify my thinking. Listening to others with a research agenda similar to mine but with a different perspective or theoretical frame assisted me to think beyond my current study.

The language used to describe change should be carefully chosen so the reader is not misled or the data incorrectly interpreted (Saldaña, 2003). Words such as adjectives and adverbs can be dynamic and placed on a continuum—for example *boring* to *fun*, *enthusiastic* to *burned out*, as opposed to the more mundane *a little* to *a lot*. However, words can mislead. For example, the adjectives *haphazard* and *flexible* convey different meanings. For example, apparent differences in implementation of a program can be attributed to a participant's action as haphazard (hit or miss) or flexible (adaptable).

Trustworthiness of Researcher's Interpretation Over Time

The researcher's interpretation of data collected is paramount. However, a study spanning years can be problematic because of the time between each data set collected and the final accumulated massive data amount. In a longitudinal study, each phase of data collection is checked for interviewees' agreement with the interview's content. During data collection, the researcher can use member checking or communicative validation (Flick, 2014). Participants can read each of their interviews and verify for accuracy of interpretation. However, in longitudinal qualitative studies, such reading involves an abundance of pages. To avoid this burden, during the 5 years of interviewing principals, I provided key drafts to participants for reaction in lieu of checking each interview. I asked for checks on only what I considered significant publications for two reasons: (1) I worried that reading what I wrote might influence future interviews; (2) busy principals in my study had little time to read academic journal publications. However, I let them know that publications were available if they were interested.

Coresearchers can also be a source of checking objectivity. Large-scale qualitative longitudinal studies are frequently conducted by multiple researchers. Thus, an additional data-accuracy check occurs when researchers independently analyze the data and discuss interpretations as the following excerpt from an article illustrates:

A quarter of all interviews were read individually by team members. Coding schema emerged from joint discussions of the individual codes. Upon agreement, codes were then applied to the remaining interview data. We engaged a similar process of coding and analysis for observation data. We first deductively coded the data and then relied upon inductive coding. In addition to triangulating methods (e.g., published course offerings in school documents), research team members independently examined the same data, which were then checked by team members for consensus. We also entered school documents in a spreadsheet so we could compare, for example, published accounts of course offerings with student transcripts.

Source: Stich, A. E., & Cipollone, K. (2017). In and through the urban educational "reform churn": The illustrative power of qualitative longitudinal research. *Urban Education,* 1–27. doi: 10.1177/0042085917690207

Flick (2014) provides a comprehensive overview of methods for checking a qualitative study's validity and trustworthiness. In a qualitative longitudinal study, these fundamental methods need special attention because of the study's longer duration. Each stage of a study provides an opportunity for accuracy checks. Before the research begins, a pilot study can enhance trustworthiness. Evaluating interview protocols through a pilot study is common. However, in a longitudinal study, a pilot study could be mandatory because the instrument will likely be used repeatedly over a long time. During the study, peer readers and reviewers can also check validity. I have benefitted from the insights of journal peer reviewers and my university colleagues as they questioned portions of my drafts. Their comments caused me to read my study more closely and to substantiate weak claims. Lastly, exit strategies, such as final interviews or participants' reading a manuscript, allow participants to reflect over the years and provide an additional check of researcher interpretation. Most discussion of qualitative studies' validity and trustworthiness focuses on data collection and analysis. Taking a different path, Patton (2002) notes that researcher credibility and trustworthiness are other dimensions of a credible study. In my review of longitudinal researchers, I found a cadre of authors whose many publications can be read in top-tier journals. They have earned respect for professional integrity and methodological expertise. Quality improves with the quantity of credible research published in highly regarded journals. My advice to new professors and emerging student scholars is that their first study should take as long as necessary to be published in a top-tier journal. The first publications are the beginning of a chain of rigorous scholarship and recognition as a competent scholar. After a rigorous first process, subsequent studies and manuscripts will be easier.

Writing the Longitudinal Manuscript

The final longitudinal manuscript must be more than an uninspiring report of events. A large data set requires extra effort to create a document that resonates with others. Writing the final manuscript is easier if the writer enjoys telling a story, is a competent writer, and favors reflection and creativity. Sometimes bright students with a sound study fall short as they write the final product. They need to be reminded that even good content is meaningless if not clearly written for the intended audience. This advice might sound strange to the researcher who views research as a science through the lens of positivism. In discussing the debate between scientific writing versus persuasive rhetoric, Flick (2014) notes that a blurring might occur between science and literature when persuading readers of a certain perspective. On the other hand, Glesne (2016) views researchers as cocreators of the story reflecting on their experiences, feelings, and interactions with participants and the research site. Kavale (1996) advises the qualitative researcher to treat interview transcripts as "living," as conversations rather than merely transcripts reducing data to a collection of words. The transcript becomes an interpretative tool, whereby the researcher can relive what was said. Kvale suggests that a key question in analyzing and writing is *"How do I go about finding the meaning of the many interesting and complex stories my interviewees told me?"* (author italics, p. 179). Furthermore, Kvale views the interview as an interaction between two persons that continues in the analysis and that is subsequently written. According to Kvale's view of analysis, the researcher focuses on the narrative, not on the collection of statements in a transcript; in other words, the researcher reconstructs the original story into a story for the audience. If this view appears to be unscientific, that is Kvale's intention. Analyzing and constructing meaning in qualitative analysis are not technological, fixed methods but methods subject to interpretation. Kvale believes that no standard method corresponding to statistical analysis exists. Instead, general approaches suffice for analyzing meaning. I have seen beginning scholars search for the *right meaning* and over the *correct version*. Instead, longitudinal qualitative analysis is highly interpretive and can be examined through multiple frameworks (Glesne, 2016). For me, thinking deeply to examine and understand the significant challenges of change in my field can be both vexing and energizing—vexing because the struggle to explore longitudinal change requires investing time in reading, reflecting, and rewriting; energizing because examining change over time can potentially solve social problems.

Peer review comments on a manuscript are an excellent source of guidance on meaningfully writing. In my qualitative longitudinal research, most peer review comments have been about the discussion section in which findings are interpreted. As a new researcher, I did not appreciate the peer reviewers' criticisms. Only after closely examining the comments' intentions did I understand that another perspective was helpful. Many authors spend extraordinary time on the findings sections as seen in the many detailed quotations from interviews. However, it is in the discussion that the researcher explains the results and assists the reader in understanding the central message. The following excerpt from a peer reviewer's comments illustrates this point:

> More than half of the article presents extensive findings in a descriptive way, followed by a very minimal discussion and analysis. Although the findings present a wealth of rich data, these need to be edited to ensure a more balanced and critically reflective discussion and analysis. I would encourage the authors to link more strongly the findings and the interpretations with the literature. This aspect is rather weak. But with some effort this can easily be rectified.

The following comment reminded me that the analysis links the interviewees' initial story "told to the researcher and the final story told by the researcher to an audience" (Kavale, 1996, p. 184): "The discussion is about answering the question. What do the findings mean? So what?"

On the other hand, a researcher might be taken to task when stepping outside the boundary. For example, one of my peer reviewers commented, "There is some 'causal' inference going on here that is calling me to call into question the claim," reminding me that a researcher's explanation cannot inflate, overinterpret, or unjustifiably speculate about the findings. Balancing these two perspectives fairly is not always easy but is necessary. Although I did always agree with the comments of reviewers, their recommendations required and deserved consideration. The following excerpt from a review is followed by my comment to my coauthor:

> *Peer reviewer:* When coming to discussion and conclusions, the authors would not need to essentially repeat the data but could demonstrate how and in what ways the trends observed in their study cohere with those from the broad range of relevant research in their review of literature on the implementation of innovations, assessment/evaluation of teaching, and leadership conducted in urban schools.

> *My comment:* I thought we did a pretty good job connecting discussion of findings to the research lit review. We could perhaps

reorganize to put our big bold assertions first in a paragraph. In our final submission, we extensively reorganized to briefly summarize the findings; connect them to the literature review; and most importantly, discuss emerging trends using words such as *perhaps*, *as seen in*, *tying together* to avoid undue speculation.

This section's purpose is not to expose reviewer bias, nor to feel good through catharsis. Instead, it is to illustrate that even experienced researchers and writers face critical reviews of their work. Such criticism is necessary to protect the research's integrity and credibility, particularly when the researcher is interpreting a large data set obtained in a qualitative longitudinal study. As Flick (2014) notes, "The text becomes the central element for judging the translation of experiences into constructions and interpretations" (p. 515). When an article is resubmitted, most journals require a response to the comments, another strategy for reflecting more deeply on the study's meaning.

A Resource

My university's library has a SAGE video collection containing 480 clips of researchers discussing and showing how methods are applied in research projects. Cases applying the methodology are also included. Although qualitative longitudinal methods are not listed, there are many other methods that would be helpful to a student, a researcher, or an instructor. For example, videos related to authors and methods cited in this book are available, including discussions of focus groups, theoretical frames, and ethnography. Furthermore, the SAGE collection discusses every research phrase including writing the final manuscript, emphasizing discussion section's importance. As an instructor, I found the transcript accompanying the video to be useful. Although the SAGE video collection might be unavailable in some libraries, a 30-day free trial is available for discovering this resource's potential.

Chapter Summary

By studying change and its effect on policy and practice, a longitudinal researcher can benefit society, organizations, and individuals. Conveying the message of change requires words that evoke feeling and that transform data to a powerful narrative. Attention to publication requirements and care to neither overgeneralize nor incorporate bias are also essential. The challenges are great, but the benefits are greater.

Reflection Questions and Application Activities

- What else would you like to know about the publication process?

- What barriers do you see in the publication process, and how might you overcome them?

- In pairs, read an article from the reference list or one your instructor provides. Summarize key words and phrases evoking a clear image of change, longitudinality, and participants' feelings.

8

CONCLUSION: LEGACIES, LESSONS, AND CHANGE

In this chapter, the reader will

- understand the importance of leaving a legacy,

- learn lessons from an experienced qualitative longitudinal researcher,

- review a checklist for conducting a qualitative longitudinal study, and

- consider the research future of stored longitudinal qualitative data.

LEAVING A LEGACY

A passion to understand change drives qualitative longitudinal researchers. Such understanding will continue beyond the study, and planning for continuation is an element of responsible longitudinal research. Researchers invest time and energy in conceptualizing a study, collecting and analyzing data, and writing the results for publication. However, organizing and maintaining the study's details are essential for future researchers to continue the work. For example, new methods might emerge for reexamining and reusing the data requiring access to the previous study details (White & Arzi, 2005). This documentation is akin to leaving an audit trail—a detailed account chronicling the researcher's thoughts and allowing others to examine how the study was conducted and the data were analyzed (Merriam, 2016; Patton, 2002; Rossman & Rallis, 2012). In published studies, this information is usually condensed. However, future researchers need more details to build on original studies.

I learned to be more intentional about leaving a legacy of information when researchers, seeking to build on my 1993 and 2009 studies of aspiring female superintendents, contacted me 8 years following the last study and I could not locate key pieces of information. The journals in which my studies were published did not require including the survey. Although I had it, I did not have all the data analysis details. Luckily, sufficient information was available, allowing researchers to continue building on my work. Fortunately, electronic storage tools simplify the process of retaining data making the problem of missing information less likely today. Regardless of the system a researcher creates, others may build on the original work, adding to a longitudinal view of change.

LEARNING FROM A DIARY OF LESSONS

The following traces the lessons I learned in doing a qualitative longitudinal study. At the end of this section are points reflected in this diary to keep in mind when doing such research.

Year 1

The state implemented a new teacher-evaluation system at the same time I moved to Tennessee. As a former evaluator of teachers and a supervisor of principals, I was keenly interested in how the system changes would affect principal practice and teacher development over time. A solid grounding in basic qualitative methods guided my thinking about a longitudinal study. Already familiar with a study's major steps (e.g., coding, theming, ethical considerations, and selecting participants), I quickly began designing the interview protocols related to my research questions. All studies select participants, but I was asking mine to participate for 5 years. New to the geographic area, I thought it might be difficult as an unknown professor to get past the gatekeepers. I also wondered if I had sufficient knowledge of state policy to frame my study's background. However, I fortuitously met a local school district assistant superintendent who was solidly grounded in the teacher-evaluation system changes. He became my valuable research partner and frequent coauthor, providing insights and inspiration.

Year 2

Through interviews, I discovered that sufficient change was indeed unfolding as a result of the state's implementation of a teacher evaluation policy. I used policy and change frameworks to analyze how principals' perceptions either changed or remained the same. Additionally, the state's new policy resulted in not only new implementation mandates but also a potentially significant effect on principals. For example, the state created policies allowing districts to align teacher salary with evaluation ratings. These new policy additions prompted me to add to the eleven interview questions one or two different questions each year, thus allowing principals to respond to the current hot topic. At this point, I published two studies of the teacher evaluation's initial implementation. Although I was becoming acquainted with the work of a few longitudinal qualitative scholars cited in this book, I had not discovered the enormous power and potential of a qualitative longitudinal approach to studying change.

Year 3

I understood how my multiyear study had the potential to improve teacher evaluation policies. Furthermore, 3 years was longer than other researchers had studied teacher evaluation; thus, I began my most prolific publication agenda. Recognizing the importance of a sustainable research agenda, I knew that teacher evaluation would always be both a supervisory and a policy issue in schools. Moreover, this topic of deep interest and concern motivated me to work through the difficult or tedious moments in a project. I spent countless hours with colleagues discussing state policy changes, reading evaluation articles, presenting at conferences, and refining my thinking about teacher-evaluation change and its long-term impact.

Year 4

I was treading familiar ground and my thinking appeared repetitive; thus, I needed to dig deeper to get the most from the data by learning more about analyzing qualitative longitudinal data. However, my search of textbooks on qualitative research yielded little more than a paragraph on qualitative longitudinal analysis. I also discovered that studying change is like the ongoing change process itself; it is an emotional roller coaster of satisfaction and frustration. At times, serendipitous insights are uncovered but frequently dead ends are encountered after a lengthy search. I began to understand that a big definitive solution for solving the dilemmas of teacher evaluation was an unrealistic goal. To spur thinking, I reread Saldaña's 2003 book and was inspired by his advice to the researcher, "expect to revise assertions continually, since data located in the future will influence and affect assertions developed in the past" (p. 93).

Year 5

After successfully probing the yearly data, I had more to analyze and to understand but was limited in strategies for digging deeper. Perhaps immersion in the study's topic had created overfamiliarity with and repeated views of the same patterns. John, my frequent coauthor, called me one day and said, "There is so much in this data we need to dig into, but we aren't getting at it. We need a fresh set of eyes and a different approach." As a result, we turned to NVivo as a method for digging deeper into the data; however, it was not an easy tool to learn. Several meetings with university data experts and attempts at independent analysis added to demanding job responsibilities and slowed the process.

I also enlisted additional people for a fresh perspective. A recently hired assistant professor in my department led to a new collaboration. Unfamiliar with my study's context, he asked questions that caused me to think in different ways. In addition, an eager and technologically savvy graduate assistant helped to move the work along. I also applied for and received a second internal grant to fund a graduate student in systematically reviewing and recoding all data.

Next, I began thinking about the many ways I could still use the data to understand change in teacher evaluation. For example, I continued developing conference presentation proposals and manuscript submissions. In the peer review feedback, significant interest in longitudinal qualitative studies was expressed. I also began realizing that longitudinal qualitative studies are rare in some academic disciplines. At this point, I understood the barriers and benefits of a scholarship agenda that embraced a long-term study. Thus, I challenged myself to compile all that I had learned to assist others; in the process, the concept of this book was born. In writing this book, I learned another lesson—I am part of a growing community of scholars sharing insights and experiences with others seeking to learn.

CHECKLIST OF LESSONS

- Be solidly grounded in qualitative methodology and then build on that knowledge with longitudinality.

- Read articles for examples of qualitative longitudinal methods used in studies.

- Be attentive and ready to identify emergent significant change study possibilities.

- Select a research topic that motivates and inspires a desire to understand change.

- Find a colleague or critical friend who is interested in sharing the long and sometimes lonely longitudinal journey.

- Look for additional theoretical frameworks or lenses for data interpretation.

- Regularly analyze and interpret the data.

- Be prepared to continually monitor change events related to your study.

- Seek feedback through peer-reviewed presentations and manuscript submissions.

- Be prepared to encounter a plateau in both motivation and data collection.

- Use the slow times to rethink, reread, and recharge.

- Select a sustainable topic and apply different perspectives to create new insights.

- Seek new methods, people, and strategies when the going gets tough.

- Be resourceful and look for ways to fund your project. Even a small internal grant can kick-start a stalled study.

- Preserve all your data.

- Persist, knowing that you are leaving a legacy for others to build on and continue a study of change.

Future Possibilities

The United Kingdom has electronically stored qualitative data generated through grants and regional archives as well as in museums throughout the country. There is interesting material on the topic to be found at https://www.ukdataservice.ac.uk/get-data/other-providers/qualitative.

Stored qualitative data opens new possibilities for qualitative longitudinal studies. A researcher can use the stored data set and apply new research questions similar to quantitative method's use of big data sets. Another possibility for researchers is collaborating on a similar topic and accessing each other's data sets. Although skeptical regarding participants' privacy and the importance of context in a qualitative longitudinal study, I am intrigued with the possibility of a new qualitative longitudinal frontier.

Chapter Summary

The qualitative longitudinal researcher has an opportunity to assist others through observations and publications of change and its effect. Writing about their study's impact, Stich and Cipollone (2017) noted that had data collection ended after 1 year, scheduling obstacles and the extent to which they act as barriers to student success would have been unobserved. Remaining in the school for a longer time revealed the deleterious morale effects of constant turnover and uncertainty.

Thus a qualitative longitudinal data set is more than the sum of its parts; it provides insights beyond those of a one-off study (McLeod & Thomson, 2009). Understanding change is central to a qualitative longitudinal study and the researcher's quest to document change effects on organizations, individuals, and policy. Yes, there are challenges; but in my experience, those are easily overcome with persistence, resourcefulness, and a desire to be part of potential solutions to contemporary problems.

Reflection Questions and Application Activities

- Interview a qualitative researcher about the challenges and benefits of longitudinal qualitative research. As a group, generate interview protocols. Bring the interview data to class for analysis and discussion.

- Take two minutes to write an "aha moment" you had after reading this chapter. Share with a partner the significance of this insight.

- A researcher designed a study examining the implementation of a new organizational initiative. The protocol specified interviews with supervisors and the implementers to understand employee perception of the initiative's effectiveness following 6 weeks of implementation. Redesign this study to incorporate qualitative longitudinality and an understanding of changes that occurred.

REFERENCES

Anfara, V. A., & Mertz, N. T. (2015). *Theoretical frameworks in qualitative research* (2nd ed.). Thousand Oaks, CA: Sage.

Barley, S. R. (1990). Images of imaging: Notes on doing longitudinal field work. *Organization Science, 1*(3), 220–247.

Bolger, N., & Laurenceau, J.-P. (2013). *Intensive longitudinal methods: An introduction to diary and experience sampling research.* New York, NY: Guilford Press.

Burgelman, R. A. (2011). Bridging history and reductionism: A key role for longitudinal qualitative research. *Journal of International Business Studies, 4*(5), 591–601.

Corden, A., & Millar, J., (2007). Qualitative longitudinal research for social policy: Introduction to themed section. *Social Policy & Society, 6*(4), 529–532.

Creswell, J. W. (2003). *Research design: Qualitative, quantitative, and mixed methods approaches* (2nd ed.). Thousand Oaks, CA: Sage.

Derrington, M. L. (in press). Principals as local actors in supervision. In S. Zepeda & J. Ponticelli (Eds.), *The handbook of educational supervision.* West Sussex, England: Blackwell/Wiley.

Derrington, M. L. (2014). Teacher evaluation initial policy implementation: Principal and superintendent perceptions. *Planning and Changing, 45*(1/2), 120–137.

Derrington, M. L., & Campbell, J. W. (2015). Implementing new teacher evaluation systems: Principals' response to change and calls for support. *Journal of Educational Change, 16*(3), 305–326.

Derrington, M. L., & Sharratt, G. C. (2009a). Self-imposed barriers. *The School Administrator, 8*(66), 18–21.

Derrington, M. L., & Sharratt, G. C. (2009b). Female superintendents: Breaking barriers and challenging life styles. *Delta Kappa Gamma Bulletin: International Journal for Professional Educators, 75*(2), 8–12.

Deutsch, M. (1992). Kurt Lewin: The tough-minded and tender-hearted scientist. *Journal of Social Issues, 48*(2), 31–43.

eSchoolNews. (2014). *Nominate your tech-savvy superintendent.* Retrieved from http://www.eschoolnews.com/resources-4-2/superintendents-center/tssa/nominate/

Flick, U. (2014). *An introduction to qualitative research* (5th ed.). Thousand Oaks, CA: Sage.

Gall, M. D., Gall, J. P., & Borg, W. R. (2010). *Applying educational research: How to read, do, and use research to solve problems of practice* (6th ed.). Boston, MA: Pearson.

Galloway, L., & Kapasi, I. (2015). How not to do it!! A salutary lesson on longitudinal and qualitative research approaches for entrepreneurship researchers. *International Journal of Entrepreneurial Behavior & Research, 21*(3), 489–500.

Giaever, F., & Smollan, R. K. (2015). Evolving emotional experiences following organizational change: A longitudinal qualitative study. *Qualitative Research in Organizations and Management: An International* Journal, *10*(2), 105–133.

Glesne, C. (2016). *Becoming qualitative researchers: An introduction* (5th ed.). Boston, MA: Pearson.

Gray, M. A., & Smith, L. N. (2000). The qualities of an effective mentor from the student nurse's perspective: Findings from a longitudinal qualitative study. *Journal of Advanced Nursing, 32*(6), 1542–1549.

Hall, G. E., & Hord, S. M. (2015). *Implementing change: Patterns, principles, and potholes.* Boston, MA: Pearson Education.

Hammersley, M., & Traianou, A. (2012). *Ethics in qualitative research.* Thousand Oaks, CA: Sage.

Hebenstreit, C. L., & DePrince, A. P. (2012). Perceptions of participating in longitudinal trauma research among women exposed to intimate partner abuse. *Journal of Empirical Research on Human Research Ethics, 7*(2), 1556–2646. doi:10.1525/jer.2012.7.2.60

Hill, G., McDonald, T., Derrington, M. L., & Calderone, S. (2017, April). *Women and the superintendency: Results of a 23-year study.* Presentation at the Washington Association of School Administrators Women's Conference, Chelan, WA.

Honig, M. I. (2006). Complexity and policy implementation: Challenges and opportunities for the field. In M. Honig (Ed.), *New directions in education policy implementation* (pp. 1–23). Albany: State University of New York Press.

Howe, K. R., & Dougherty, K. C. (1993). Ethics, institutional review boards, and the changing face of educational research. *Educational Researcher, 22*(9), 16–21.

Hsieh, H.-F., & Shannon, S. E. (2005). Three approaches to qualitative content analysis. *Qualitative Health Research, 15*(9), 1277–1288.

Jacob, S. A., & Furgerson, S.P. (2012). Writing interview protocols and conducting interviews: Tips for students new to the field of qualitative research. *The Qualitative Report, 17*(6), 1–10.

Johnson, R. B., & Christensen, L. (2014). *Educational research: Quantitative, qualitative, and mixed approaches* (5th ed.). Thousand Oaks, CA: Sage.

Kearney, K. S., & Hyle, A. E. (2015). A look through the Kübler-Ross theoretical lens. In V. Anfara & N. Mertz (Eds.), *Theoretical frameworks in qualitative research* (pp. 110–129). Thousand Oaks, CA: Sage.

Knapp, M. S. (2017). The practice of designing qualitative research on educational leadership: Notes for emerging scholars and practitioner–scholars. *Journal of Research on Leadership Education, 12*(1), 26–50.

Kotter, J. P. (1996). *Leading change.* Cambridge, MA: Harvard Business Review Press.

Kotter, J. P. (2012). *Leading change.* Boston, MA: Harvard Business Review Press. (Original work published 1996)

Kübler-Ross, E. (1969). *On death and dying.* New York, NY: Touchstone.

Kvale, S. (1996). *InterViews: An introduction to qualitative research interviewing.* Thousand Oaks, CA: Sage.

Lewin, K. (1952). *Field theory in social science: Selected theoretical papers by Kurt Lewin.* London, England: Tavistock.

Lewis, J. (2007). Analyzing qualitative longitudinal research in evaluations. *Social Policy and Society, 6*(4), 545–556.

Lomascolo, D. J. (2016). *Principals' perceptions of the Tennessee teacher tenure law: A concurrent mixed methods study* (Unpublished doctoral dissertation). University of Tennessee, Knoxville.

Maxwell, J. A. (2005). Qualitative research design: An interactive approach. Thousand Oaks, CA: Sage.

McCoyd, J. L., & Shdaimah, C. S. (2007). Revisiting the benefits debate: Does qualitative social work research produce salubrious effects? *Social Work, 52*(4), 340–349.

McLeod, J., & Thomson, R. (2009). *Researching social change.* Thousand Oaks, CA: Sage.

Merriam, S. B. (2009). *Quantitative research: A guide to design and implementation* (3rd ed.). San Francisco, CA: Jossey-Bass.

Merriam, S. B., & Tisdell, E. J. (2016). *Quantitative research: A guide to design and implementation* (4th ed.). San Francisco, CA: Jossey-Bass.

Miles, M. B., & Huberman, A. M. (1994). *Qualitative data analysis* (2nd ed.). Thousand Oaks, CA: Sage.

Miles, M. B., Huberman, A. M., & Saldaña, J. (2014). *Qualitative data analysis* (3rd ed.). Thousand Oaks, CA: Sage.

Miller, T. (2015). Going back: "Stalking," talking and researcher responsibilities in qualitative longitudinal research. *International Journal of Social Research Methodology, 18*(3), 293–305.

Mills, M. R., & Bettis, P. J. (2015). Using multiple theoretical frameworks to study organizational change and identity. In V. Anfara & N. Mertz (Eds.), *Theoretical frameworks in qualitative research* (pp. 96–118.). Thousand Oaks, CA: Sage.

Mintrop, R., Ordenes, M., Coghlan, L. P., & Madero, C. (2018). Teacher evaluation pay for performance and learning around instruction: Between dissonant incentives and resonant procedures. *Educational Administration Quarterly, 54*(1), 3–46.

Morrison, Z. J., Gregory, D., & Thibodeau, S. (2012). "Thanks for using me": An exploration of exit strategy in qualitative research. *International Journal of Qualitative Methods, 11*(4), 416–427.

Neale, B., & Flowerdew, J. (2003). Time, texture and childhood: The contours of longitudinal qualitative research. *International Journal of Social Research Methodology, 6*(3), 189–199.

Newman, E., Willard, T., Sinclair, R., & Kaloupek, D. (2001). Empirically supported ethical research practice: The costs and benefits of research from the participants' view. *Accountability in Research, 8*(4), 309–329.

Novak, J. D. (2005). Results and implications of a 12-year longitudinal study of science concept learning. *Research in Science Education, 35*, 23–40.

Okilwa, N., & Barnett, B. (2017). Sustaining school improvement in a high-need school: Longitudinal analysis of Robbins Elementary School (USA) from 1993 to 2015. *Journal of Educational Administration 55*(3), 297–315. doi:10.1108/JEA-03-2016-0034

Patton, M. Q. (2002). *Qualitative research & evaluation methods* (3rd ed.). Thousand Oaks, CA: Sage.

Peck, C., & Reitzug, U. C. (2017). Discount stores, discount(ed) community? Parent and family engagement, community outreach, and an urban turnaround school. *Education and Urban Society, 49*(5), 1–22.

Pinnock, H., Kendall, M., Murray, S. A., Worth, A., Levack, P., Porter, M., . . . & Sheikh, A. (2011). Living and dying with severe chronic obstructive pulmonary disease: Multi-perspective longitudinal qualitative study. *BMJ, 342*, 1–10. doi:10.1136/bmj.d142

Richardson, J. W., & Sterrett, W. (2018). District technology leadership then and now: A comparative study of district technology leadership from 2001–2014.

Educational Administration Quarterly. Advance online publication. doi:10.1177/0 013161X18769046

Robards, B., & Lincoln, S. (2017). Uncovering longitudinal life narratives: Scrolling back in Facebook. *Qualitative Research*, *17*(6), 715–730.

Rossman, G. B., & Rallis, S. F. (2012). *Learning in the field: An introduction to qualitative research* (3rd ed.). Thousand Oaks, CA: Sage.

Saldaña, J. (2002). Analyzing change in longitudinal qualitative data. *Youth Theatre Journal*, *16*(1), 1–17.

Saldaña, J. (2003). *Longitudinal qualitative research: Analyzing change through time*. Walnut Creek, CA: Altimira Press.

Saldaña, J. (2015). *Thinking qualitatively: Methods of mind*. Thousand Oaks, CA: Sage.

Saldaña, J. (2016). *The coding manual for qualitative researchers*. Thousand Oaks, CA: Sage.

Sharratt, G., & Derrington, M. L. (1993). Female superintendents: Attributes that attract and barriers that discourage their successful applications. *Management Information*, *13*(1), 6–10. Retrieved from http://files.eric.ed.gov/fulltext/ ED362941.pdf

Stich, A. E., & Cipollone, K. (2017). In and through the urban educational "reform churn": The illustrative power of qualitative longitudinal research. *Urban Education*, *52*(2), 1–27. doi:10.1177/0042085917690207

Taris, T. W. (2000). *A primer in longitudinal data analysis*. Thousand Oaks, CA: Sage.

Thomson, R., & Holland, J. (2003). Hindsight, foresight and insight: The challenges of longitudinal qualitative research. *International Journal of Social Research Methodology*, *6*(3), 233–244.

Thomson, R., & McLeod, J. (2015). New frontiers in qualitative longitudinal research: An agenda for research. *International Journal of Social Research Methodology*, *18*(3), 243–250.

Utley-Smith, Q., Bailey, D., Ammarell, N., Corazzini, K., Colón-Emeric, C. S., Lekan-Rutledge, . . . & Anderson, R. A. (2006). Exit interview-consultation for research validation and dissemination. *Western Journal of Nursing Research*, *28*(8), 955–973.

Vallance, R. J. (2005, September). *Working with longitudinal qualitative data: Using NVivo as an analytic tool*. Paper presented at the 6th International Strategies in Qualitative Research Conference, Durham University, Durham, England.

Weis, L., Eisenhart, M., Cipollone, K., Stich, A. E., Nikischer, A. B., Hanson, J., . . . & Dominguez, R. (2015). In the guise of STEM education reform: Opportunity structures and outcomes in inclusive STEM-focused high schools. *American Educational Research Journal, 52*(6), 1024–1059. doi:10.3102/0002831215604045

White, R. T., & Arzi, H. J. (2005). Longitudinal studies: Designs, validity, practicality, and value. *Research in Science Education, 35*(1), 137–149.

Winkler, I. (2013). Moments of identity formation and reformation: A day in the working life of an academic. *Journal of Organizational Ethnography, 2*(2), 191–209.

Winkler, I. (2017). Doing autoethnography: Facing challenges, taking choices, accepting responsibilities. *Qualitative Inquiry, 23*(8), 1–12. doi:10.1177/1077800417728956

APPENDIX

Picturing Policy Implementation:
An Ethnography of a Local Network.
A case study by Pam Carter.
Published on SAGE Research Methods,
Online ISBN: 9781526432063,
DOI: http://dx.doi.org/10.4135/9781526432063
©2018 SAGE Publications Ltd.

ABSTRACT

Ethnography involves "being there" as a witness in a particular field. This unusual form of social interaction can feel uncomfortable but the opportunity to gather rich qualitative data in real time is a major strength of the method. Limitations of ethnography are that this method is restricted to particular situations—there will always be practical constraints on ethnographers in terms of how much time they have to devote to immersion in a particular field. This case examines ways in which a local policy network made sense of its task of implementing a project linked to an early years childcare policy. The case demonstrates how ethnography showed the network juggling creatively with time and money and making sense of its task using pictures and other artifacts. Project management is a rational linear approach that usually regards time and money as fixed resources, but this study revealed how the future was creatively symbolized, how time sped up toward the financial year-end, and how resources were variously presented as meager or plentiful. Power relations meant that the project manager who took responsibility for the time-tabled targets thereby controlled much of the network's activity. The case sets out the importance of theory when analyzing data; in this case, the analysis transformed mundane objects into sociological artifacts and "made the familiar strange."

PROJECT OVERVIEW AND CONTEXT

This case study derives from a doctoral research project that used an ethnographic approach to study at a local level how the United Kingdom's early years childcare policy shift from Sure Start to Children's Centres took place. Policy implementation has been considered to be a "black box" as policy directives often fail to translate into practical outcomes and ethnography offers a valuable research method for opening up the black box to study the complex and messy process of implementation. In this case, a local authority took the decision to create multiagency networks that it termed "Community Learning Partnerships" to build on the Sure Start programes and create new Sure Start Children's Centres. Whereas Sure Start had mainly been about physical buildings for childcare, parenting support, and early years development, Children's Centres moved toward "campus models," rebranding existing Sure Start Centres, and often designating community nurseries and other facilities as "Sure Start Children's Centres." Initially, my PhD study explored gender and class issues around welfare-to-work initiatives and what I saw as the potentially contradictory aim of supporting parents in their role of caring for their children. My analytical interest in time, money, and project management was not anticipated at the outset but emerged inductively through the stages of fieldwork, data analysis, and writing up.

RESEARCH PRACTICALITIES— GETTING IN AND GETTING ON

Before I could collect data, I needed to obtain ethical approval from what was then the National Health Service (NHS) research governance system. This was time-consuming and at times felt like trying to fit the square peg of an ethnographic iterative study design into the round hole of the NHS expectations of informed consent and a study protocol (Murphy & Dingwall, 2007). Following my attendance at a local ethics committee and the completion of a host of mandatory research governance documentation, permission was granted. I explained that I would seek permission in advance from the chair of meetings to observe the committee's routine business. The chair could then seek consent from people who were due to attend the meetings, and if there were objections, I would not attend. Inevitably, once I got into the field, reality was more complex than predicted by the plan detailed in ethical procedural documents.

Gaining access to the field was relatively straightforward as I drew on my "social capital" (Edwards, 2004). I had previously worked in local government and health and started with some initial contacts, which then snowballed. I asked the Chair of a local network for permission to attend its meetings as a nonparticipant observer and made sure that study information leaflets were on hand for anyone who queried my presence. In practice, I established a relationship of trust over time and sought to blend in. At network meetings, it was fairly easy to merge into the background, sitting alongside people I was observing and scribbling my fieldnotes because others who were attending also took notes at meetings. The experience of nonparticipation observation was not straightforward, however. Sometimes I became aware that people sitting next to me were interested in my notes, so I tried to shield them. I needed to make judgments "on the hoof" about where to sit and how much to say. Sometimes I found myself behaving more like a participant-observer. For example, I volunteered to help with refreshments, partly as a means of gaining trust and through wanting to seem useful. At one network meeting where votes were being cast by means of raised hands, I was asked why I was not voting. On one hand, I was flattered that I had become accepted. On the other hand, conscientiously, I reminded people that I was not there as their equal but as a researcher. Hannabuss (2000) writes about the ethnographer being the research instrument him- or herself and certainly this is not a method for the fainthearted! The ethnographer needs to establish and maintain fieldwork relationships so that he or she can gather naturalistic data, but he or she must also remain alert to what Willis and Trondman (2000) have called "aha" moments. These are moments where the background noise of fieldwork can be distinguished from data that signal theoretical significance. Theory is what takes ethnographic research beyond what otherwise could seem like journalism.

RESEARCH DESIGN AND METHOD IN ACTION

In contrast to experimental studies that test hypotheses, ethnographic study designs are usually emergent and exploratory (Bryman, 2012). My data collection plan could not be clearly specified in advance but needed to iterate and depended partly upon opportunities that arose when I was in the field. For example, I heard about an early years childcare conference and requested permission to attend. There I heard speeches and sat through various presentations about local multiagency networks. Presentations were invariably positive about the future, encouraging people attending the conference to "get on board" with the plans to deliver Sure Start Children's Centres via Community Learning Partnerships. At lunchtime, I browsed the information stalls and I was particularly interested in one that displayed a series of laminated slides depicting a project journey using a cartoon image that showed passengers boarding a school bus. Consistent with the rhetorical emphasis on the positive, at the end of the metaphorical journey, was a picture of a rainbow and an overflowing crock of gold. The slides seemed to have been designed to convey a linear project "journey," leading to plentiful resources that could be spent on the particular defined goals of the network. I asked the person behind the information stall whether they would be willing to send me an electronic version of the slides to use in my research and they generously agreed. As well as the pictorial slides, I gathered other artifactual data in the form of a giveaway toy, a teddy bear wearing a vest that promoted the local authority childcare service (Carter, 2011).

"Stuff" is important in social life and tends to be neglected by researchers (Appadurai, 1998), but ethnography offers the opportunity to see how social actors use material objects and visual representations to make sense of and interpret their version of reality. Sense-making is not only an activity that sociologists do but is a basic human practice as Weick (1995) has shown. My research used the pictures and artifacts produced by these actors as research data, and I went on to analyze these as alternate local representations of national policy implementation.

Following the conference, I maintained my presence in the local network for about 8 months, during which time the network allocated resources to a variety of projects, including equipment for an after-school club, family learning activities at the local college, resources for schools, and so on. A project management framework was put in place by the local authority, imposing expenditure targets on local networks to ensure quick decision-making. I interviewed several key people confidentially but found that people often gave me the "official version" of policy, conforming to the notion of rational implementation. In contrast to this relatively banal data, I found ethnography very useful for getting beyond the "official line" (Duke, 2002) and for observing what people *do* that may be different than what they are prepared to say. For example, often in interviews, people would espouse the benefits of the policy and were reluctant to criticize reductions in funding. The illustration of peanuts that I observed showed that, in practice, there were acknowledgments that resources were meager, especially when compared with initial expectations.

It was vital for me to preserve confidentiality as I interviewed several people face to face as individuals and then also encountered them in meetings. Sometimes I needed to give vague responses when I was questioned "Have you interviewed so-and-so?" At other times I explained that I couldn't reveal who had taken part in interviews. At the end of interviews, I would often reassure interviewees that if I were to subsequently encounter them in meetings, I may appear to ignore them. Rather than this being rude behavior, it was necessary to preserve confidentiality. This meant that sometimes I avoided eye contact with individuals while at the same time staying alert and maintaining an interest in the meeting discussions. Emotional labor is thus part of an ethnographer's task and Hannabuss (2000) provides a useful discussion of this process of "being there."

At one early meeting, a slide presentation by the local project manager had a different tone to the rhetoric of optimism that I had observed at the conference and was more pragmatic about the reality of what could be achieved by local networks. For example, rather than the crock of gold, the manager showed an image of peanuts in their shells to convey what, to them, were interpreted as meager resources. During these meetings I became increasingly aware that the financial year-end was approaching, and decision-making seemed to speed up and become somewhat frenetic to avoid project "underspend." At the last meeting I attended, the project manager explained that the committee had the flexibility to allocate their time to different budgets (*vire* is the accounting term for moving money between different budget headings). Thus, if the project budget was under-spent, the committee would charge more of its time and so retrospectively adjust the budget to fit. This enabled members to present the project as a success in terms of milestones achieved.

ANALYZING DATA
AND WRITING UP

Ethnography can generate large amounts of data. I had what felt like masses of interview transcripts, fieldnotes, policy documents, and artifacts. I published some articles relatively quickly on the theme of welfare reform, policy "initiativitis," and longer-running social structures. It took me much longer to write up the academic article on time tactics and to do so I needed to consider a new research question and apply fresh theory in order to make sense of the remaining data. I had a hunch, a feeling—untheorized initially—that there was something interesting about the contrast between the crock of gold and the image of peanuts, and I had experienced an "aha" moment when the project manager told the network she could charge back her time. I read and selectively made use of Adam's (2013) work on timescapes, Pollitt's (2008) work on time and management, and Foucault's work on governmentality and discipline (Foucault, 1980, 2003). These theories eventually helped me to see how, in the data, time appeared to be both mundane and metaphysical. Project management assumes a linear notion of time and tends to presume that time and money are fixed resources. In contrast, fieldwork revealed that there were different interpretations of the available resources as either plentiful or parsimonious (crock of gold or peanuts). Time, rather than being measured in strict clock time, seemed to speed up toward the end of the financial year but also was reversed when the manager retrospectively accounted for time allocated to the project.

In the published article, I included the pictorial slides that I had collected at the conference but I removed identifying features. I also included several quotes extracted from interview data, as well as selected data based on my handwritten field notes. I wrote part of the article in the present tense in an attempt at achieving a sense of immediacy for the reader.

PRACTICAL LESSONS LEARNED

Research governance procedures can appear cumbersome and bureaucratic, but it is important for ethnographers to conduct their research ethically. In this case, having an information sheet to hand out meant that if I was questioned about my presence, I could produce a justification for being in particular fieldwork situations and provide contact details for anyone with further questions.

Ethnographic fieldwork generated a large amount of data that presented challenges but could be used to write up articles later. Theory is vital—reality is not simply "out there" to observe and represent in any objective fashion and so reflective time away from the field is vital for getting to grips with academic literature that can aid data analysis.

As long as ethical considerations and copyright conventions are complied with, journal editors are willing to reproduce photographs and images within research articles.

I advise student ethnographers with interests in policy and practice to exercise their sociological imagination to look out for the "aha moments" (Willis & Trondman, 2000) when policy rhetoric may contrast sharply with local implementation practices.

EXERCISE

1. Making the familiar strange
   Students should bring an object into a group discussion. Objects might be ones that are easy to collect or that have particular meaning in their lives. "Found objects" could be a pebble, leaf, or a nonnatural object such as a coffee cup. Artifacts such as an identification badge or part of a uniform might relate to professional life. Some may be ephemeral such as a paper napkin, others more symbolic such as a family photograph. Students should be prepared to discuss how the objects came into their possession, what practical use (if any) the objects have, any surprising features, and what personal memories are associated with the images/objects.

   The aim is to "make the familiar strange" and the object of the exercise is to stretch the sociological imagination to consider the multiple meanings that might attach to objects and the ways in which they relate to a social context. Students at an advanced level of qualitative research might engage with actor network theory (Callon, 2007) to consider who these objects enroll in what ways.

2. Observational skills and ethical reflexivity
   Students could practice their observational skills in a social setting such as a train station, library, canteen, or park. They should

consider recording methods and practice taking fieldnotes. They should be prepared to discuss ethics and how this exercise made them feel—perhaps like covert spies, investigative journalists, trainee ethnographers, or other. They should exchange observations and challenge one another to think about what they have taken for granted, how their perceptions frame reality, and what they may not have fully observed. Links with theory are to be encouraged so that observations are linked to academic debates and the generation of new research.

EXERCISES AND DISCUSSION QUESTIONS

1. When might nonparticipant observation become uncomfortable, and what strategies might be adopted in fieldwork?

2. Explain the role of artifactual data.

3. What do you think the ethnographic method added to interview data?

4. Why do ethnographers need to theorize when they analyze observational data?

FURTHER READING

Clifford, J., & **Marcus, G. E.** (1986). *Writing culture: The poetics and politics of ethnography*. Berkeley: University of California Press.

Hodder, I. (1994). The interpretation of documents and material culture. In **J. Goodwin** (Ed.), *SAGE biographical research* (Vol. 1, pp. 171–188). London, England: Sage.

Atkinson, P. (2015). *For ethnography*. Thousand Oaks, CA: Sage.

WEB RESOURCES

Multimodal ethnography
http://www.cardiff.ac.uk/socsi/hyper/pubs.html

100 social objects
https://www2.le.ac.uk/projects/social-worlds

REFERENCES

Adam, B. (2013). *Time and social theory.* Hoboken, NJ: Wiley.

Appadurai, A. (1988). *The social life of things: Commodities in cultural perspective.* Cambridge, England: Cambridge University Press.

Bryman, A. (2012). *Social research methods.* Oxford, England: Oxford University Press.

Callon, M. (2007). Some elements of a sociology of translation. In **K. Asdal, I. Moser,** & **B. Brenna** (Eds.), *Technoscience: The politics of interventions* (pp. 57–78). Oslo, Norway: Unipub.

Carter, P. (2011). Governing welfare reform symbolically: Evidence based or iconic policy? *Critical Policy Studies, 5,* 247–263.

Duke, K. (2002). Getting beyond the "official line": Reflections on dilemmas of access, knowledge and power in researching policy networks. *Journal of Social Policy, 31,* 39–59.

Edwards, R. (2004) *Social capital in the field: Researchers' tales* (Families & Social Capital ESRC Research Group, Working paper No. 10.) Retrieved from https://www.lsbu.ac.uk/data/assets/pdf_file/0003/9444/social-capital-families-research-working-paper.pdf

Foucault, M. (1980). *Power/knowledge: Selected interviews and other writings, 1972–1977.* New York, NY: Pantheon Books.

Foucault, M. (2003). Governmentality. In P. Rabinow & N Rose (Eds.), *The essential Foucault: Selections from the essential works of Foucault, 1954–1984* (pp. vii–xxxv). New York, NY: New Press.

Hannabuss, S. (2000). Being there: Ethnographic research and autobiography. *Library Management, 21,* 99–107.

Murphy, E., & **Dingwall, R.** (2007). Informed consent, anticipatory regulation and ethnographic practice. *Social Science & Medicine, 65,* 2223–2234.

Pollitt, C. (2008). *Time, policy, management: Governing with the past.* Oxford, England: Oxford University Press.

Weick, K. E. (1995). *Sensemaking in organizations* (Vol. 3). London, England: Sage.

Willis, P., & **Trondman, M.** (2000). Manifesto for ethnography. *Ethnography, 1,* 5–16.

INDEX

Made in the USA
Las Vegas, NV
29 January 2022

42525303R00075